Dedication

In Memory of

Eleanor

26th June 1944—1st March 1994

Hushed is the world from toiling

Quiet from fret and care

Evening has spread its shadows

In sunset and twilight air

Table of Contents

HMS Ganges

Inscribed upon a plaque at the entrance to the gymnasium, this poem best describes the goal instructors sought to achieve from young boys passing through that now long disappeared training establishment.

IF

If you can keep your head when all about you
Are losing theirs and blaming it on you,
If you can trust yourself when all men doubt you,
But make allowance for their doubting too;
If you can wait and not be tired by waiting,
Or being lied about, don't deal in lies,
Or being hated, don't give way to hating,
And yet don't look too good, nor talk too wise:

If you can dream—and not make dreams your master,
If you can think—and not make thoughts your aim;
If you can meet with Triumph and Disaster
And treat those two impostors just the same;
If you can bear to hear the truth you've spoken
Twisted by knaves to make a trap for fools,
Or watch the things you gave your life to, broken,
And stoop and build 'em up with worn-out tools:

If you can make one heap of all your winnings
And risk it all on one turn of pitch-and-toss,
And lose, and start again at your beginnings
And never breath a word about your loss;
If you can force your heart and nerve and sinew
To serve your turn long after they are gone,
And so hold on when there is nothing in you
Except the Will which says to them: "Hold on!"

If you can talk with crowds and keep your virtue,
Or walk with kings—nor lose the common touch,
If neither foes nor loving friends can hurt you,
If all men count with you, but none too much;
If you can fill the unforgiving minute
With sixty seconds' worth of distance run,
Yours is the Earth and everything that's in it,
And—which is more—you'll be a Man, my son!

Rudyard Kipling (1865-1936)

Acknowledgements:

I extend a very special thank you to my friend B Gerad O'Brien.

A great Irish writer with a love and talent of story telling

His best selling books include

'Once on a Cold and Grey September'
&
'Dreaming Dreams'

Special thanks to my sister-in-law, Alma Birt, for her valuable assistance in the Editing this book

Chapter 1
Kippers for Breakfast

It was Tuesday, the fifteenth of March 1955. I was aboard the Belfast to Liverpool steamer, one of six new Royal Navy recruits en-route to HMS Ganges. Crossing the Irish Sea from Belfast had been unusually calm. Perhaps it had something to do with the misty overcast weather.

Still, I was grateful for a flat sea, it would have been embarrassing to be seasick on my first day as a sailor. Not that other passengers would have noticed, to them I must have appeared as just another silly young boy.

During the last hour of the crossing I'd stood alone at the ship's guardrail daydreaming. I imagined myself on the bridge of a warship. A stalwart seaman, feet firmly planted on a pitching deck, binoculars at the ready searching for an enemy fleet.

The ship's foghorn suddenly sounded overhead, breaking my salty reverie. The ship was slowing as it neared the wharf at the Albert Docks. My five companions joined me on deck and we watched the Liverpool skyline gradually materializing through the fog.

Twenty minutes later the gangway was in place and passengers began to disembark. Six young Jolly

Jacks finally set foot on a Liverpool jetty, thus ending the first part of our epic journey.

Our next task was to find the seaman's mission where we were to spend the night before travelling on to London the following morning. The address was clearly listed on the sheet of instructions given to us by the recruiting officer in Belfast.

After asking a dockworker for directions we set out on foot to find it. Having no luggage to carry we decided to walk and save on bus fares. I almost regretted this decision because on leaving the dock area, I spotted a line of trams. They were parked in front of a huge building. At the time I assumed it was the City Hall but I later discovered that it was the Mersey Port Authority Building.

The sight of the trams rekindled fond memories of the old Belfast trams that were taken out of service in 1952. They had for years been my favourite mode of travel. The Liverpool trams were the same familiar Chamberlain models but in their drab green paint didn't look nearly as grand as my Belfast trams.

Now wasn't the time to reminisce about the past. I had far greater priorities on this important day.

We continued down the main street taking in the sights and sounds of the unfamiliar city. Ten minutes later, on the opposite side of the street, we spotted the mission sign on a two-storey red brick building.

One of the boys noticed a cinema a couple of doors down. The feature film was George Orwell's '1984', and he suggested we should go there after supper.

At the mission we were assigned beds, issued with pillows, blankets, towels and soap. The menu for tonight's supper was bangers and mash, tea and rice pudding. We were informed that it wasn't served until 6 pm. So having an hour or so to kill we decide to test our bunks and rest up before eating. We smoked cigarettes talked and laughed at silly jokes.

We were nervous, anxious and impatient to move on to the next stage of our adventure. We agreed after supper that we *would* go to the cinema; it would help pass the time. It was a strange film about an imagined world some thirty years in the future that I didn't particularly enjoy. I had little interest or comprehension in such a futuristic world. 1984 was just too far in the distance to think about.

The sleeping quarters in the mission was a large dorm containing approximately thirty beds. We cautioned each other to sleep with our wallets under our pillows. Liverpool was a busy seaport and the mission was filled with a variety of merchant seamen from many lands. In fact our sleep was disturbed several times during the night by late arrival of somewhat drunken sailors. I was introduced to a sleeping environment of loud and differing sounds of snoring, farting and belching. However, sharing space with so many bodies was something I would soon become accustomed to in my chosen career.

I arose around six the next morning and headed to the communal bathrooms to wash and brush my teeth. There was very little movement at that early hour; most of my neighbours were still sleeping soundly.

Trevor Weir, a wee lad from Ballymena appeared shortly after me and we finished our ablutions together. We dressed and returned our bedding to the used-linen hampers provided. With twenty minutes to go before breakfast, Trevor suggested we take a walk around the block and have a smoke.

Outside, the morning air was crisp and clear, and there were few people about as we sauntered down the street puffing on Woodbines. My companion, as nervous as me, started a conversation about how he imagined life would be at Ganges, but neither of us came close to picturing what lay in store for us once we passed through those barrack gates.

As we returned to the Mission a clock was chiming the hour from somewhere in the city. I was hungry now and my thoughts turned to a hearty breakfast of bacon and eggs, toast and a large mug of tea. We entered the dinning area where the four other recruits were already in line waiting to be served. Trevor and I collected our cups, plates and cutlery from a table at the side of the counter then we lined up behind them.

When my turn came I held out my plate and the cook dumped something on it that I didn't recognize. He was a big burly man who didn't look particularly happy with his lot in life so I decided not to ask him what it was and I joined my friends at the table.

We had all been served the same thing, and I wasn't the only one who didn't know what it was. Fortunately one boy did, and he informed us that we each had a pair of smoked kippers. I was no wiser, but I was equally sure that it was something I'd not normally eat for breakfast. Or at any other meal, for that matter. So I had to content myself with bread, margarine, marmalade and a cup of tea.

I soon learnt that kippers were a popular item on the Navy's breakfast menu, and they were better known in Naval terms as 'Spithead Pheasant.'

With our less than scrumptious meal finished we collected our coats and departed the mission. Lime

Street Station wasn't far away, so again we decided to walk and conserve our dwindling funds. We had ample time; the London train didn't leave until 8.30am.

The next leg of our journey began with a five-hour train ride to Euston Street Station in London. Six of us clambered into an eight-seat compartment just behind the engine. In the fifties, British Rail still used the old style carriages that had no corridor linking the compartments. Passengers were confined until the next station. It was incumbent on one to use the public lavatory before embarking on the train. The next stop could be hours away, and the duration of the stop at the station was often too short to make it to the toilet and back. Stops could last anywhere from two to five minutes, there was really no way of knowing.

Of course, in desperation, one could always use the window.

This was only an option if the compartment contained only your shipmates. At best, it was risky, requiring careful aim and timing. The wind rushing past the window could cause an embarrassing spray, known as getting your own back.

It was also a risk racing to the station cafeteria for a cuppa and bun. It usually meant competing with dozens of other passengers doing the same thing, and it always seemed that just as I was being served the whistle would blow, signalling that the train was leaving. With rising panic, and trying not to spill several mugs of tea, came the mad dash back to the carriage. The train moving and gathering speed, I'd pass the mugs to outstretched hands while running alongside, finally managing to scramble on board, as the end of the platform loomed large.

This same operation would be repeated many times during my Naval career, though in later years it would be pints of beer rather than tea, I became quite competent in platform racing, and though I had some close calls I never actually missed a train.

The journey to London was uneventful, and we arrived safely at 1.30 pm on Wednesday afternoon. The next part of our schedule was tight. The train to Ipswich departed at 3.45pm, and we needed to navigate through the London Underground System to Liverpool Street Station.

The underground is indeed an amazingly simple system, and even fools like us found our way without mishap. At Liverpool Street Station we sought out platform fourteen to begin the final leg of our journey.

At the gate we saw dozens of boys milling around and we knew instantly that we'd arrived at the right place. There were close to a hundred boys of all shapes and sizes. The air on the platform was filled with their noisy chatter and laughter.

On the train I sat beside a boy who looked closer to twelve than fifteen. His name was Jameson and he was joining from the Royal Hospital School at Holbrook, the same place where I had almost ended up in1952. He went by Jamie, and though we couldn't know it then, we would be shipmates for the next three years.

During the journey to Ipswich everyone in the compartment talked excitedly and constantly. On arrival, the carriage doors flew open to discharge their eager cargo. We had arrived.

Several Petty Officer Instructors from Ganges were there to meet us, and it quickly became evident that it was not to roll out a welcome mat! Suddenly we were being yelled at, told to shut up and sort ourselves into three neat lines. This was my first taste of Naval discipline.

Over the next twelve months, forming three neat lines would become a way of life. We marched smartly out of the station. Well, we thought we were smart. Several dark blue lorries with canvas covers were lined up in the parking area. Emblazoned on the cab doors in large white letters was RN.

In an orderly fashion we were loaded into the vehicles, and the convoy set out for the base at Shotley village. The cold and uncomfortable drive took about twenty minutes.

Sitting in the back of a covered lorry, you only see where you've been, not where you're going. So when the lorry made a right turn, I was surprised to see a huge ship's mast with a white ensign flying from it. Below the mast was what looked like the main entrance to HMS Ganges.

I was confused. It appeared we going in the wrong direction, away from the camp. Suddenly we entered a smaller camp, and the lorries circled wide and stopped.

The next instant our world exploded with yelling, shouting and blowing whistles. In confusion and fear, we rapidly evacuated the trucks to land on a parade square. Petty Officers attempted to organize us into a division of three neat rows. I noticed several uniformed boys wearing white gaiters and, like the POs, appeared to have authority over us. In fact they were doing most of the shouting and shoving.

"Three rows, you idiots! Tallest on the ends shortest in the centre. Move, move, move!"

Once we were formed into three ragged lines, silence descended. A Chief Petty Officer and several Petty Officers stood in front of us with clipboards.

"Listen carefully," the Chief Petty Officer said. "When your name is called, fall out and go to the Instructor Boy on your left."

So that's who these guys in the white gaiters were, Instructor Boys.

By the time everyone's name was called we'd formed three separate groups. Only one of the six lads from Belfast was in my group. Being separated from my travelling companions caused me an anxious moment. It didn't last long, though. Things were moving too rapidly.

The camp, I later learned, was known as the Annex. The buildings were formed evenly around the parade square. At the top end were the Instructor's quarters, along with an area known as the quarterdeck. I would soon learn that the quarterdeck was a very sacred part of ship. When entering this area, we had to salute and double smartly across it. The mast, a ship's bell and two ancient cannons identified it.

To the left was the guardhouse, plus two accommodation blocks. Facing the mast at the other end of the parade square was the mess hall, the showers and the laundry rooms. On the right was the last of the accommodation blocks, and it was to become my home for the next six weeks.

Our group was ordered to turn left and march in single file into our mess block. To achieve this single file, two Instructor Boys shoved and pushed us, calling us stupid in a variety of Naval terminology. Once inside, we were told to stand at attention beside a bed, no talking, no moving. The Petty Officer who had called out our names entered the block and told us to stand at ease.

"My name is Petty Officer Birmingham. For the next six weeks I shall be the most important person in your life. At all times you will address me as Sir, and you will only address me when I say you can. Instructor Boys Mathers and Moss will be in charge when I'm not here. They too, will be addressed as Sir."

I was beginning to wonder why we'd been told their names. Obviously we'd never be allowed to use them. The Petty Officer gave us a brief outline of what lay ahead, and what was expected of us in the coming weeks. When he'd finished there wasn't a boy who was not scared. Perhaps a few were even terrified

Instructor Boy Moss told the boys on the left to turn right and follow him in single file.

Those of us remaining were told to sit on the long bench in the middle of the mess. We were handed a pencil, some paper and an envelope, then ordered to write a brief letter letting our parents know we'd arrived safely.

By the time our letters were completed, the other group was returning. They carried bedding and clothing; piled so high it was difficult to see where they were going. Then it was our turn to march out in single file behind Instructor Boy Mathers. We marched into a supply room where the clerks, giving us a quick onceover, decide what size clothing we needed. In rapid order we moved along the supply line, and the issue of blankets, pillow and clothing grew ever larger. We marched in single filed back to the mess to join the rest of our group as they finished their letters. The next order took everyone by surprise, and caused us considerable embarrassment.

"Strip! Everything off, underwear, socks, the lot! Put everything on your mattress, and stand by you beds again."

Twenty-seven red face boys stood stark naked, trying not to look at each other. The senior Instructor Boy held up a pair of newly issued white underpants. He told us to find ours and put them on. Next he held up a vest. Embarrassment receded as we dressed by number.

Within two minutes we were clothed in our work uniforms, which are known as Number 8's. We looked a sorry sight; every item of clothing was stiff and ill fitting. I'd always imagined myself as a dashing figure in my smart new uniform. What I was wearing now was not smart or dashing. In the following weeks, washing our kit over and over again, the new unworn look soon disappeared. As my skill with an electric iron improved, I soon began to look a little smarter too.

On that first day we were told to gather all our civilian clothes for packing. We packed every item, socks, underwear, and hankies—the lot.

When the pile of brown paper packages and the stack of one page letters were addressed and ready, four boys were detailed to collect them and follow Instructor Boy Moss.

Those remaining were told to march in single file to the washrooms, wash our hands then fall in three deep outside the mess hall. It was now almost 1900 hrs as we were marched into the mess hall for supper. There were no cooks on duty. The Annex wasn't officially operational until the following morning. We were issued with mugs of kye, (cocoa) bread, margarine, cheese and jam.

When the meal was over it was back into three lines to march back to the accommodation block where we were told to strip again! It was shower time. Very cold shower time.

I was learning that there was neither modesty nor privacy in the Navy. The shower room had about eight or ten showerheads, and twenty-seven boys were told to get under the freezing water and wash. Included in our newly issued kit was a large bar of soap. It was called Pusser Hard, and it was used for washing everything, including me.

In the showers, a few boys barely got wet before dashing for the exit. But dodging a cold shower was not possible. Petty Officer Birmingham stood at the exit, waiting to inspect each one of us. If he decided a boy wasn't clean, it was back under the showers.

Shivering badly, we quickly dried ourselves with our newly issue waterproof towels. Then we marched in single file back to the mess with towels around waists and we stood by our beds.

"You have thirty seconds to get into your pyjamas," was the next order.

Quietly and quickly, we complied. We were freezing. A bed was dragged to the centre of the mess and Instructor Boy Moss demonstrated the Navy's method of making up a bed.

The owner of the demonstration bed was greatly disappointed when it was pulled apart again. We were learning that *nothing* would ever be done for us.

It took ages to conclude the exercise. Instructor Boys marched up and down, pulling beds apart that didn't meet standards. Finally everyone achieved the requirements, and twenty-seven exhausted boys turned in.

It was 2100 hours, time for lights out. We were given a final stern warning not to talk. Just one sound and everyone would be on the parade square for an hour of doubling.

Utter silence fell on the place. I lay quietly in my bed, gazing at the rafters. I was tired but very happy. I had arrived. Thus ended the first day of my Naval career.

Chapter 2
The Annex.

My pleasant and dreamy sleep was suddenly invaded by the glare of lights and the shrill sounds of whistles blowing hysterically. It seemed like I'd only just gone to sleep a few minutes earlier and now I was out of bed and standing at attention.

A few heavy sleepers, or perhaps they were just trying to avoid the inevitable, remained under their covers. It was a bad idea. Beds were quickly flipped over, empting blankets and bodies onto the deck.

Instructor Boys loomed over the hapless late sleepers issuing dire threats of punishment. The most unpopular of these punishments was to double around the parade square with your rolled up mattress on your back.

After that first morning everyone became light sleepers. We were out of bed the instant we were called.

At 0500 hrs on that dark and chilly Thursday morning we were ordered to wash and shave. It mattered not that most of us didn't need to shave. It was wiser to do what we were told without objection.

Everyone lathered up and with our newly issued razors removed imaginary stubble, bum fluff and peach fuzz. Shaving for the first time was made even more difficult by the fact that the water was very cold.

By five-thirty we were stripping our beds and folding the bedding. Like the night before, this was a long-suffering exercise. Once more, our two Instructor Boys paraded up and down the mess throwing blankets and sheets on the deck that failed to meet the required standards.

The bedding finally folded in a uniform state we were ordered to dress in our number eights with boots and gaiters. Number eights consisted of dark blue trousers, light blue shirt, boots, gaiters and cap. We were issued with a pair of khaki gaiters that set us apart from the Instructors who wore white gaiters.

Out on the parade square the first rays of daylight were appearing as we separated into two squads. Instructor Boy Moss was in charge of my squad. I was glad. Of our two young mentors he was the more gentle. Although gentle probably isn't the best word to describe any Instructor Boy.

Boys spilled out of the other two barracks to join us on the parade square. It was drill time! Drill requires total concentration, listening carefully to each order that was issued by the Squad Leader. The exercise was made doubly difficult by having six separate Squad Leaders all yelling similar orders at the same time.

The next hour was spent marching, doubling, turning left, turning right, and about turning. It was a disaster. Few boys appeared to know their left from their right. This sent the Instructors into a frenzy of more dire threats.

At 0700 hrs we were dismissed and told to form a single line outside the dining hall for breakfast. We were very hungry. Our last meal had been a meagre supper of bread and cheese. Added to this was the early morning hour of rigorous drill. We had become a ravenous hoard.

When I finally reached the food counter I surmised that the cook must be related to the one at the Liverpool Seaman's Mission. My plate once more held a mystery food. It turned out to be kidneys on toast better known in Naval terminology as 'shit on a raft'. I'd never tasted a kidney in my life, but with a powerful hunger I swallowed every bit washing it down with generous gulps of tea. I finished breakfast by polishing off several thick slices of bread, margarine and marmalade.

Breakfast was followed by a hectic morning. We collected the remainder of our kit and we had to stamp our name on every single article.

At the same time haircuts were taking place on the parade square. Several barbers (boys in training) from the main establishment were doing the shearing. I doubt any of them would have been hired to shear sheep. Supervision came from two disinterested civilians who I assumed were qualified barbers. The parade square was a scene of lost curls and locks with occasional traces of blood. When it was over selling Brylcreem or a comb would have been impossible.

Through the course of the morning we learned that we were to remain in the Annex for six weeks. It was necessary to undergo basic training before moving to the main establishment to begin the actual seamanship training.

Boys in the Annex were known as Nossers, a somewhat detrimental name applied to newcomers and rookies.

During basic training our names had to be sewn into each article of kit with a red cotton chain stitch. To accomplish this task we'd been issued with a sewing kit, better known as a 'housewife.' A great many boys would spend every free minute of the next six weeks with their 'housewife.' No one could leave the Annex until the sewing was completed. No one wanted to be left behind to start all over again with the new intake.

In our naïve and simple minds we believed that once we reached the main establishment things would get easier.

Four particular things stand out in my memory of the Annex. Sewing and folding, washing and marching. Marching and marching. I believe we spent more time on the parade square than we did in bed.

Our first visit to the laundry was a severe shock for everyone. Hand washing our kit with 'pusser hard' soap was an experience none of us could have imagined. I suspect that the laundry and the sewing were a nightmare for many boys. The boys with long surnames suffered the sewing chore more than most.

However, many boys with short names who were woefully inept with a needle didn't fair much better. Our Instructor Boys inspected each item of kit, and often made us cut the thread out again and redo it. I can't remember the exact number of articles in a Naval kit but at the time it seemed like hundreds.

The most unpleasant experience in the Annex, and the one I consider a blemish on an otherwise fair training system, was the laundry. Ganges training was indeed very harsh and it's true that sometimes the Instructors went too far. Nevertheless, if you carried out your duties properly you could generally stay out of trouble.

The Annex laundry was a different matter. The person in charge was a civilian named Knobby Clark.

It was rumoured that he'd once been a Royal Marine Corporal. If this was true it did nothing to enhance my image of the Marines. He was a bully and tyrant deriving pleasure from picking on the smaller boys in our division. He carried a sail baton and used it liberally and mostly without cause on many a bare buttock of his hapless victims.

His golden rule was silence! Should a boy dare to speak he was struck maliciously and made put a wet wool sock in his mouth for the duration of the session. It was a doubly unpleasant punishment. The dye from the sock ran into your mouth and dripped into the sink. Washing your whites while avoiding the blue dye dripping on them was nearly impossible.

Each washed item was held up in front of Clark to inspect and approve. He rarely approved anything the first time around. He enjoyed grabbing the wet article and, in a swinging motion, wrapping it around the unfortunate boy's head.

He enjoyed inflicting punishment, and his face seemed permanently fixed in an evil grin. I no longer remember his actual features but retain an image of an unshaven, overweight bully with a half-smoked butt in the corner of his mouth. Looking back, it's disappointing that our Instructors didn't step in and take control. It will forever stand out as a serious blemish on the Ganges organization. To employ such an ill suited person and placing him in a position of authority over defenceless boys was, to say the least, shameful. From that dreadful laundry experience I have often wondered if the term 'put a sock in it' originated at Ganges.

Beside my bed was a kit locker. Its doors were always open displaying my (hopefully) neatly folded kit.

A photograph of how the kit locker was supposed to look was placed on the mess notice board. Our lockers were supposed to look identical. Unfortunately many lockers failed to meet the standard and, like our beds, were often tipped over.

Once a week we had a full kit inspection. All kit items had to be laid out on our canvas hammock. Every article of clothing must be folded to the same length and width as our seamanship manual. The sewn on names had to be centrally located on each folded item. Spit and polish was soon added to an already overwhelming list of chores. Petty Officer Birmingham expected to see his face in the shine of our boots. Dawn to dusk was filled with work. If we found a spare minute it was used to complete our sewing.

A variety of other training events were happening at the same time. The mess hall was cleared one afternoon and a boxing ring set up. We were paired up regardless of size, and ordered to punch each other's lights out.

On a cold and windy April morning we were ordered to strip to the waist and form three single lines on the parade square. I was covered in goose bumps with my teeth chattering as we waited in line for inoculations!

I still shudder at the methods employed back then. Three tables were set up at the end of the parade square. At each table sat two Sick Bay Ratings (nursing assistants of a sort). On each table was a Bunsen burner that was used to sterilize the needle after each use. The same needle was used on approximately thirty to forty boys. We were lined up in alphabetical order. For those at the rear, which included me, the blunt needle felt more like a six-inch nail being driven into one's arm.

We were never given more information than necessary during our day- to-day training in the Annex. So imagine our surprise when a rumour began to circulate that we were going on leave the following week.

I couldn't believe it. Three weeks in the Navy and we were going on leave. It just didn't seem possible. Nevertheless, it was true. The following Wednesday the entire camp was closing down for three weeks Easter leave.

The news was both good and bad. It was exciting to be going home wearing our uniforms. However, it was a serious interruption to training just when we were adapting to the harsh routine. Going on leave could mean having to start all over again when we came back. It was also a temptation for any unhappy lad to attempt desertions.

Organizing the leave of hundreds of boys and dispatching them to different locations across the nation was a grand example of Ganges efficiency. Everyone was separated into local zones; my group consisted of approximately thirty boys going to Northern Ireland.

A handful of boys from the South of Ireland had to travel in civvies. It was considered unwise to wear the Queens uniform South of the border.

Ipswich Station thronged with young sailors looking for space on the trains. Almost everyone travelled to London then fanned out and disappeared into various tube stations.

On the train I was amazed to see many of the boys from the main establishment busily sewing a variety of badges onto their tunics. They exchanged their Ganges cap tallies for those of sea going ships. We

Nossers from the Annex sat apart in our plain and obviously brand new uniforms.

Nozzers were considered wet behind the ears and boys from the main establishment ignored us. Sailors for barely three weeks, we had yet to learn the trick of looking smart and natty in our new uniforms. Boys from the main establishment had learned to bleach their blue uniform collars. After many washes the collar turns a lighter shade of blue, and it was the sign of an old salt. My own collar, along with my companions, was dark blue. In fact it was almost black.

During my time at Ganges I would see many a collar ruined with bleach and a variety of other experiments used to lighten the colour. I would surmise that the purchase of uniform collars from slops (Supply) was an item high in demand.

My first shore leave as a sailor was very quiet, and it required the constant explanation as to why I was home so soon after joining. Besides, having only been in the Navy for one payday, I had very little money to spend. Three weeks later I was back in the Annex to complete my basic training before moving on to the main establishment. When that big day finally arrived we were divided into our new divisions and introduced to our new Instructors.

I joined Drake Division, and I was allocated to number 40 Mess. We were further divided into two separate classes, number 16 and 17.

Our new Instructors were Petty Officers Booty and Russell. They would soon prove to be much harder on us than the ones we were leaving behind.

Chapter 3
The Main Establishment

Drake division was located at the top of the short covered walkway, and Number 40 Mess was almost directly under the huge mast, just opposite the base Post Office. Trevor Weir was the only one from our original Belfast six still with me. Where everyone else had gone to I had no idea.

Training now took on a much greater variety of subjects, and the swimming test was amongst the first, and the hardest, to pass. The test entailed staying afloat for twenty minutes in the deep end of the swimming pool whilst wearing a canvas duck suit. Any boy who grabbed onto the side of the pool failed immediately and was listed as a backward swimmer. I was lucky, and I passed first time. But I have to tell you, wearing a canvas suit makes the job very difficult because the canvas quickly becomes waterlogged and extremely heavy, making swimming very tiring.

To be listed as a backward swimmer was not good. If you were one of those unfortunate boys, it meant you had to attend the pool every morning at 0500 hours for thirty minutes of swimming. The early hour and cold water made your life very unpleasant. Sunday was the only day you were excused.

However, it also proved an effective training strategy because the boys were motivated to become stronger swimmers very quickly.

Like the Annex, we seemed to spend more time on the parade square than we did in bed. Petty Officer Russell was our drill and gunnery Instructor, and he put us through a series of exercises. We learned how to crew and fire a four-inch gun, a common weapon on most of our warships at the time.

We were taught how to function in a gas filled environment with our gas mask removed.

On the range we practiced firing the Lee Enfield .303 rifle. This rifle had a violent recoil action and it could cause a nasty shoulder injury if it was held incorrectly, so we quickly learned how to hold them properly. During the range training I qualified for my first badge, the Marksman Cross Rifles badge. I was very proud.

Petty Officer Booty taught us seamanship, tying knots, splicing ropes, and rigging a block and tackle. We learned the alphabet of the semaphore code, which at the time began Able-Baker-Charlie-Dog etc, and was use for signaling at sea. But it seemed we had no sooner learned this system than it was changed to the international code of Alpha-Bravo-Charlie-Delta etc. Such was the life of a young sailor in training. We had no choice but to get on with it.

Before sun-up we would pull (row) a 32-foot Naval cutter up and down the Orwell River, racing cutters from the other divisions. To lose a race was unacceptable to our instructors, and it usually resulted in us doing extra time on the river. We learned how to sail a 27-foot whaler, and we often missed supper while trying to sail across the wind in a hopeless attempt to return to the jetty on time.

Sunday was hardly a day of rest at Ganges. It began with the whole camp on parade. Dressed in our Number Ones, which was our best uniforms with gold badges, we marched smartly past the Saluting Dais, following the guard, the boys bugle band and the band of the Royal Marines.

After the parade we lined up to attend Church services, and how the Navy decided who attended which Church has always remained a mystery to me. We were divided into three groups, the Church of England, Roman Catholic and the Free Church of Scotland. Anyone who didn't belong to the first two churches had to attend the Free Church.

On Sunday afternoon we were free to climb the mast, play sports, or, if we had any money, go into Ipswich where we could stay until 1900 hours. But few of us had money so we spent our time sitting on the yardarms of the 147-foot high mast, viewing the surrounding countryside.

The mast was indeed the landmark of Ganges, a spectacular sight that could be seen from many miles away. It was even more impressive when, on ceremonial occasions, it was manned by hundreds of boys in uniform. One boy, who was certainly braver than me, would stand on the button at the very top of the mast and salute. Below him on each platform, yardarm and halyards, boys manned the rigging, standing side by side with their arms and legs extended.

A total of more than eighty boys would spread out on each and every part of the mast, and it was a marvellous sight to behold.

Then, at the sound of a bugle call, and in total silence, the mast would be vacated in less than one minute.

As the year rolled on I made good progress, and in June I was promoted to Badge Boy, or Leading Boy. I was one of four with this rank in the mess, and we were in charge of everything when the Instructors were absent. We took charge of our classmates, marching them smartly about the camp, to classes, meals and wherever else we had to go. We marched everywhere. No one dared to wander around Ganges.

While I was doing reasonably well, the same could not be said for my shipmate Trevor Weir. He was constantly in trouble, as he found learning the many drills and seamanship routines very difficult.

By far his biggest problem was his dress and deportment. He always seemed to arrive on parade in a uniform that was badly in need of ironing, or a visit from a needle and thread. His unsightly appearance was guaranteed to send our Instructors into a fit of rage. This made things bad for the whole class because we were often punished as well because of *his* sloppy turn out. Trevor quickly found himself very unpopular with his messmates.

We also had a full kit inspection on a regular basis, and these were usually a disaster for Trevor. His whites had taken on a greyish hue, and, like his deportment, fell far below the expected standard.

One day, returning from my second leave in August, I was waiting at the Belfast quay when his mother approached me. She asked me to help her son and naturally I agreed. But she didn't fully understand what she was asking of me. Just keeping myself at the correct standard required was difficult enough. To help

Trevor as well was all but impossible. Of course we were encouraged to work as a team and help each other where we could, but that didn't mean washing his kit, doing his ironing, dressing him or supervising his drill. Every boy was expected to become proficient in these areas by himself. Besides, if you were caught helping someone lay out his kit for inspection you could well find yourself under punishment.

When Trevor returned from leave his whites were the envy of the whole mess. His mother had washed them until they looked as clean and pure as virgin snow. Alas, they didn't remain like that for long. All too soon they returned to their usual dull grey, and so did his troubles.

In October I was promoted to Petty Officer Boy. At about the same time a dance was arranged in the gym. Girls were invited from Ipswich and surrounding area. There was no shortage of pretty young dance partners, but the majority of boys at camp couldn't dance.

Yours truly certainly could, my many nights at the Plaza now proved most beneficial.

I asked a pretty Ipswich girl named Carol Syrett to dance and was delighted when she said yes. It was love at first sight, and we danced together the whole night.

I saved my meagre funds to visit her in town the following weekend, and we wrote to each other and exchanged photos. I even wrote home telling Anna that I was in love and thinking of getting engaged. Anna, obviously somewhat concerned, advised me that I should wait a few years.

Her advice was wise but unnecessary. Things moved too fast at Ganges for romance to blossom. Seeing Carol on a regular basis was not possible. We soon drifted apart, and I suffered the first of the many broken hearts from which I somehow always recovered. Yet it's strange that after all these years I still remember Carol, and her Ipswich address; Number 2, Pound Cottages.

Trevor's career remained on a downward spiral; he was always in trouble, suffering one punishment after another. Petty Officer Russell, our Gunnery Instructor, became so frustrated with his constant grubby appearance that he ordered him to be washed out on the parade square.

Of all the unusual things I saw at Ganges, this stands out as the cruelest and most soul destroying, of them all. A washtub was placed on the parade ground and filled with cold water. Both classes were made to participate in what followed. Trevor was ordered to strip naked and get into the tub, and we had to scrub him down with stiff scrub-brushes and 'pusser hard' soap. No one could avoid participating in this dreadful punishment. To try and dodge it meant we'd be next in the tub.

When it was all over Trevor's skin was red raw, and tears streamed down his face. The pain and torture he suffered that day was surely better suited to an older Navy of cannon and canvas. I really felt Trevor's awful agony, yet there was nothing I could do to console him.

I can't remember the exact date, but some weeks later he disappeared from Ganges. He had been discharged as an unsuitable candidate for the Navy. It was dreadful news and I felt I'd failed my shipmate.

I questioned if I could have done more. Had I tried harder, might things have turned out differently? But in retrospect, there was really nothing I could have done for him. Trevor just wasn't cut out for a life in the Navy.

As March of 1956 neared, we prepared for the completion of our year of training. Many tests and exams lay ahead, but the fear of failure was tempered with the excitement of being drafted into the fleet soon after. We speculated on where, and to which ships, we might be sent. Many rumours circulated amongst us. Everyone hoped to go to a small ship, such as a frigate or a destroyer. We were well aware that on a larger ship like a battleship or a carrier, the discipline would be a lot stricter. Discipline was something we'd had more than enough of at Ganges.

As we completed our final exams I was promoted to Instructor Boy, and I was to be sent back to the Annex for approximately fifteen more weeks. This was a double edge sword; on the one hand I was over the moon at having obtained the highest rank a boy could reach, but it meant I would not go to sea for a further three months. It also meant I wouldn't be going to sea with my classmates.

I never considered that I had a choice. I was conditioned to do what I was told and when to do it. Donning white gaiters with my uniform and packing my kit, I proudly returned to the Annex. I was teamed up with another newly appointed Instructor Boy named Jameson (Jamie). We knew each other from a year earlier when we sat together on the train from London. That seemed like a lifetime ago. But it was good having a friend to begin my new role of Instructor boy.

The Navy was modernizing and we were no longer to be called Boy Seamen. We were now Junior Seamen, thus my new title was Junior Instructor. The lengths of service also changed, although that wouldn't directly affect me until I reached my eighteenth birthday. The new terms were nine or fourteen year's continuous service. This replaced the old terms of twelve years, or seven and five reserve.

Becoming a Junior Instructor had some advantages and privileges. However, it was far from easy work. We were expected to set the highest standard at all times. Uniforms and deportment must always be impeccable. It was our responsibility to get the new recruits up in the mornings and into bed at night. This meant we were first up and last to bed. Between new intakes the Annex was deserted, and we were left to do as we pleased. Besides enjoying a well-earned rest we were free to roam about the village. We struck up relationships with the local girls. If I remember correctly there were only two. The Canteen Manager's daughter and the Church of England Padre's daughter. Naturally, great care was exercised in wooing the girls. Even with our privileged rank disaster could strike if their parents found out. I have no doubt our freedom to leave the Annex would have been instantly curtailed.

I can understand the saying 'lock up your daughters'; it surely applied to those families living beside a camp of roughly one thousand hormonal young Jolly Jacks.

Chapter 4
The Road To Singapore

In early August Jamie and I were informed that we were leaving the Annex to join HMS Whitby, which was tied up alongside in the dockyard at Devonport. It was a temporary draft; and we'd soon receive new orders. I was excited and when I asked the Senior Instructors in the Annex what type of ship the Whitby was he said it was a new frigate designed for anti-submarine warfare.

Early on the15th August, along with several shipmates, I joined my first real ship. I was immediately put to work giving the hull a fresh coat of battleship grey paint.

Within an hour of arriving I had managed to replace my cap tally for an HMS Whitby one. I consigned the Ganges tally to the depths of the murky dockyard waters.

Jamie and I had to quickly adjust to our new shipmates. For the last three months as Junior Instructors we had been saluted, addressed as Sir and generally treated with great respect. That was over now, and we'd returned to the lowly rank of Junior Seaman. However, with so many new and exciting things happening this turned out not to be a difficult transition.

Our time on Whitby was indeed temporary. On the 19th August we were told to pack our kit and be ready to move. Not a problem for me. Having only arriving four days earlier I'd not found time to unpack.

My next draft was really exciting. With roughly two hundred other draftees I was flying to Singapore to join HMS Cockade. I saw flying as an amazing adventure. Like me, few of my shipmates had ever been near an aircraft much less flown in one. There was much speculation about this, such as wondering if we would be issued parachutes. Air travel was quite rare in those days and was considered unsafe by a large segment of the population.

The Royal Navy chartered aircraft as a method of replacing a whole ship's crew while allowing the ship to remain on station. Skyways Airlines was the charter company selected for the Singapore run. They operated out of Stansted airfield. Their fleet consisted of several twin and perhaps a few four engine prop jobs with a carrying capacity of approximately fifty to sixty passengers and crew. I'm not sure what type of aircraft we flew on, possibly Handley Page or Hermes. Both were popular carriers in use with major British airlines at the time.

While packing and preparing to travel to London events in the Middle East were coming to a head. In 1956 trouble was brewing between England, France and Egypt. The major issue concerned the Suez Canal. Large forces were being concentrated in the Mediterranean and an invasion appeared imminent. Cockade's new crew, while not involved in the Middle East problem, had to pass through the area landing to refuel along the route.

The flight to Singapore was estimated to take four days with two over-night stops in Karachi and Calcutta. There were some other refuelling stops. In London we were instructed to wear civilian clothing for the flight. If we landed in a place hostile to British intentions we'd not be recognized as military personnel. Well, that was the theory though I doubt we'd have fooled anyone.

The question of wearing civvies created a problem for us boys. Civilian clothing had not been allowed at Ganges. Consequently we only had uniforms.

I no longer remember who solved this dilemma but I'll never forget that ill fitting, oversized and worn out grey suit that was issued to me. I had to turn up the trouser bottoms and gather in the waist and hold it in place with my pusser belt. The white shirt draped my diminutive upper body like a huge robe. I didn't even attempt to wear the jacket. The only article of clothing that fitted properly was my highly polished uniform boots. I wasn't alone. Poor Jamie, even smaller than me wore equally ill-fitting clothes. We were certainly a motley crowd boarding the aircraft that morning. But who cared. We were about to fly to the other side of the world.

Racing down the runway bumping and rattling was unnerving to us first time fliers. Nevertheless, we did our best to look cool and unconcerned. Finally airborne, we didn't exactly soar into the great blue yonder. It was more like a slow lumbering crawl that just managed to clear trees and buildings. I have no idea what height we levelled off at but the experience was amazing. The first leg to Brindisi took about four hours and we landed there to refuel. After experiencing a successful landing we were allowed off the plane to stretch our legs. We were not allowed inside the terminal building though.

Much later we landed in Karachi and were bussed to a local hotel. The heat was oppressive and the only cooling in our room came from a slow moving overhead fan. Jamie and I shared a sparsely furnished room of two single beds a mirror and a shower stall. We were fascinated having mosquito netting over our beds.

Trying to shower the next morning was a failure because we only managed to squeeze a few drops of rusty water from the showerhead.

The following night's accommodation was much more classy. Landing in the early afternoon at Calcutta we were driven to the Great Eastern Hotel. It was located somewhere near the city centre. It was definitely the finest hotel I'd ever seen. Our room was furnished in traditional Indian style complete with a very ornate bathtub that actually worked.

We were given strict instructions not to leave the hotel for any reason. After a wonderful meal in the grand dinning hall we returned to our rooms where we were expected to remain until morning. But it was quite impossible for six restless young men to stay in while outside a mysterious new world beckoned. Temptation finally overtook us and six greenhorns from Ganges ventured onto the street. Immediately the most amazing sights and sounds confronted us. There were people everywhere, walking, riding bikes, pulling rickshaws and availing of lots of other strange methods of transportation.

There was poverty such as I'd never seen before. People sat on the sidewalk while others slept in doorways. Throngs of half naked children swarmed us begging for money.

While absorbing this incredible scene I became aware of someone tugging my foot with the obvious intention of polishing my boots. I protested that my boots were fine and didn't need to be cleaned. Reluctant to appear rude and unsure of what I should do I let him polish them. When he finished he held his hand out for payment.

"Three pence, Sahib."

I had no small change on me except for half-a-crown, my worldly wealth at the time. I handed him the coin expecting to receive two shillings and three pence in change. But this enterprising little shoe-shiner realised it was his lucky day. Half a crown in Calcutta was a small fortune and he was unwilling to part with it. After much arguing, me in English and him in a mixture of unrecognisable words like 'me no unstandi the great Sahib,' I did finally get some change back.

It came in the form of three Player's cigarettes and sixpence. That expensive venture onto a Calcutta street barely a few feet from the hotel front steps was enough for me. Now considerably poorer I hastily returned to my hotel room.

The next day we landed in Singapore and moved into the accommodation block at HMS Terror, the local shore base. There we waited for the arrival of the rest of the crew before joining the ship the following day.

The wait was longer than expected. Two of the five planes that left England with us had broken down along the route. They finally arrived two days late. During the delay I'd almost burst with frustration waiting to see my new ship.

On a hot Thursday morning the lorries arrived and we loaded kit bags and hammocks then moved out towards the dockyard. At last I was on my way.

Ten minutes later the convoy came to a halt alongside a magnificent County Class destroyer, HMS Cockade.

The ships company divided into trades and divisions. The Seaman branch were mostly allotted messes in the forward part of the ship. Engine room personnel (still popularly known as stokers from the coal burning days) were accommodated near the mid-ship section close to the engine room. Other smaller trades like electricians were scattered throughout the ship.

The remainder of the day was mostly taken up with orientation finding a locker, stowing our kit and claiming a place to sling a hammock. As a junior sailor in the Starboard mess my choice was whatever space was left over. We met with the Divisional and Petty Officer. They handed out our watch keeping duties and told us which part of the ship we were responsible for. My part of the ship was the forecastle, a big area to paint and clean. It also seemed to have more brass fittings than any other area.

My action station was 'A' gun, the most forward of the three four-inch weapons. It was located on the fo'c's'le, (phonetic spelling of forecastle). There were two more guns. 'B' was located just below the bridge, and 'Y' was located aft.

Over the next two months we spent all our time at sea training and learning our various duties. My experience at Ganges was proving to be very worthwhile as I became adept with the many seagoing tasks.

In November of 1956 the Cockade was detailed for escort duty with the Royal Yacht Britannia. The Duke of Edinburgh was aboard and travelling to Melbourne Australia to open the Olympic games. Before the rendezvous with the Yacht it was all hands to paint ship. We had to be spic and span from top to bottom for this royal duty.

The Olympic cruise was promulgated on the ships notice board with scheduled visits to Brisbane and Sydney. Five days in Melbourne for the opening week of the games. Then off to Adelaide for a short visit. Returning to Melbourne for the final week of the games. It was the trip of a lifetime and I eagerly painted my part of the ship in preparation for the big day. I never imagined it could get any better.

But one afternoon my name was called over the tannoy (the ship's loudspeakers). I was anxious because being instructed to report to the Regulating Office was never a good sign. I must have looked worried when I arrived because the Master at Arms told me to relax.

"I understand you have a valid drivers licence,"
"Yes Sir, I do," I replied.

I was mystified as to why this would be of any importance. He explained whilst we were in Melbourne the ship would be provided with a vehicle probably a jeep. The ship required four volunteer drivers.

Wow! I couldn't believe my luck. Naturally I volunteered immediately. I was then booked to take a driver test. It was rare for a junior rating to be offered such a cushy number. but it had nothing to do with my rating. Very few of the crew could drive or had a licence.

Once four qualified drivers were found we were sent ashore to take the test. A dockyard transport manager supervised the test that wasn't too difficult. I passed and was duly issued an Admiralty driving permit.

In early November we took up escort duties with our sister ship HMS Consort and the cruiser HMS Newcastle. Arriving off the Australian coastline we were dispatched from escort duties for a three-day visit to Brisbane.

Next we sailed down the coast to Sydney arriving early on a Sunday morning. I was off duty and went ashore for a look around. I was disappointed to find everything closed and the city almost deserted. With little else to do I walked onto the famous Sydney Harbour Bridge and took a few photos. Thus far Australia had turned out a bit of a disappointment.

However arrival in Melbourne promised that was all about to change. Unlike the previous two cities Melbourne was a hive of activity. The streets and shops were decorated and the pavements teemed with huge numbers of tourist and visitors. The harbour bristled with warships from a variety of nations. An Italian cruiser was tied up near us and its huge superstructure dwarfed the lesser vessels around it.

My pressing concern was of course, the arrival of our transportation. I was anxious to know what I'd be driving. In due course a navy blue Willys jeep pulled up alongside the gangway. Painted in white on each side were the letters RN.

The other drivers and myself listened intently as the driver explained the idiosyncrasies of this unique little vehicle. It was left hand drive. Australians, like the English, drive on the right. The jeep was simple to drive and actually a lot of fun. This was definitely the best duty experienced so far in my short Naval career.

Over the next few days I was called upon to drive the Skipper to the city to meet officials or attend receptions. I also drove many of the ships officers to a variety of destinations. I had the distinct feeling we were more a taxi service than a military service.

Nevertheless, I enjoyed the job and indeed considered myself to be quite important. On the morning of the opening of the Olympic games things were quite hectic. As duty driver I'd already completed several runs in the jeep. Then around tot time a group of about eight or ten shipmates rolled off the gangway and made a beeline for the jeep. Without asking, they piled in and demanded to be chauffeured to town.

Being young and a very junior sailor I was easily intimidated by older shipmates. I knew it would be difficult, maybe impossible, to get them out of the jeep. I decided that the best course of action was to drive them to the nearest pub.

I started the jeep and headed for the city centre. This wasn't as simple as it might sound. Two of my passengers were sitting on the bonnet impeding my vision and speed. I finally reached the main thoroughfare leading to Flinders Street and ask myself why you couldn't find a pub when you so desperately needed one.

I eased the jeep in the left lane that took me to the main street. Too late I realised that it was a bad mistake. Directly in front of me was a police barrier. Too close to avoid my only option was to stop. As I slowed the jeep I was surprised to see a policeman step forward and wave me through. Immediately I found myself in the middle of a street lined with thousands of flag waving people.

In the split second it took to pass through the barrier I realised what had just happened. The policeman had assumed we were an official party sent to line the street. The second realisation caused me to break out in a cold sweat. I envisioned a court martial and being hanged from the nearest yardarm at dawn. Oh my God, I was trapped in the street that the Duke was going to travel along on his way to the official opening of the Games.

The only way out was to drive the length of the street and get off at the other end. But what if I met the Royal Entourage coming the other way? I couldn't just drive past them. I would have to back up. I would surely cause an international incident and end my brief naval career.

In the meantime my unconcerned passengers were having a ball waving enthusiastically at the spectators. Many in the crowd waved back and cheered. This only prompted my rum-sodden shipmates to reach to greater lengths of entertainment.

Not one of them gave me a thought or considered my predicament. I was having difficulty gripping the steering wheel with my sweaty palms. I drove as fast as I dared down the crowded and narrow street. Fortunately I reached the end of the street without incident and turned sharply into an alley. I'd had quite enough and turning yelled at my passengers to "get the hell out of my jeep!"

No longer a shy young sailor or afraid. I was so angry they vacated the jeep and were gone in seconds.

Being a Junior Sailor in the Royal Navy brought with it certain rigors and difficult situations. Life on board HMS Cockade was no exception. We were constantly tormented and teased. We often found ourselves doing the least pleasant jobs. To be appointed 'Captain of the Head' was not an honour. It merely meant you were responsible for cleaning the toilets.

On the seaman's mess deck we enjoyed an on-going rivalry between Senior and Junior seaman. This was my first ship so I had no way to compete with stories of previous ships. I didn't count my four days in Whitby.

Taff Richards, recently turned twenty, was old enough to receive a daily tot of rum. Tot time was the time when messmates regaled us with stories of adventure aboard their last ships. Most stories were hard to believe and were usually greatly exaggerated. It was on one of these occasions that Taff decided to tell us a story about his last ship..

His story would be remembered for the duration of our time on Cockade.

It came about when someone commented that a small tramp steamer had failed to dip its ensign when passing us that morning. Merchant ships traditionally lowered their flag when passing a warship as a salute or mark of respect.

Immediately Taff began relating a story about his last ship a Mediterranean based destroyer. He was working on 'B' gun, just below the bridge when a merchant ship passed and didn't dip its ensign. The Captain ordered the ship to turn and go after the miscreant freighter. He leaned over the bridge and shouted down to Taff.

"Put a shot across her bow, Mr. Richards".

This outlandish tale went well beyond the most exaggerated of tot time stories. No sane captain fired on a merchant ship and certainly not for so minor an offence. Poor Taff made a name for himself that day. For the next two years he was known as 'PASAHB,' an acronym for 'put a shot across her bow.'

We spent a week in Melbourne then sailed in company with the submarine Arroches, to visit Adelaide. I heard we were the first warships to visit since the First World War. Arriving on a sunny Sunday morning and not on duty I headed ashore with my shipmate Danny Gorman.

We didn't get very far because the main city was some miles away and there was no bus service on Sundays. We walked a mile or so along a dry and dusty road without seeing a soul. The place was reminiscent of a Western cowboy town complete with hitching rails in front of the few buildings we encountered. After an hour of walking we gave up and headed back toward the ship.

When the ship's mast came into view in the distance we noticed a distinct list to port. As we drew nearer we realised why we hadn't seen a soul on our trek to town. It looked like the whole population of Adelaide had come to us. The ship and the submarine were open to visitors. The line of people was close to a mile long. Our heavy list to port was due to so many people trying to visit the submarine tied up outboard of us.

We returned to Melbourne for the closing week of the Games and I was reunited with the jeep. Nothing exciting happened to me in the final week. However, another driver name Roger after driving two of our officers to a local brewery did come a cropper. At the brewery the officers were invited inside for cocktails and Roger was left waiting outside in the hot sun.

No sooner had the officers disappeared into the brewery than an employee called Roger over and began pouring him one glass of beer after another. When the officers returned Roger had to load several cases of wine and beer onto the jeep. Everything went fine and he managed to get the officers and alcohol safely back to the ship. That's when he encountered the problem.

The large quantity of beer he'd consumed was taking effect. As Roger hefted a case of wine onto his shoulder and headed unsteadily for the gangway he missed it and disappeared over the side.

Several crewmembers fished him and the wine out of the water. They managed to get him below decks and out of sight quickly. I don't think the officers noticed what had happened because they were pretty much in the same condition as Roger.

In December with our escort duties completed we sailed for the South Island of New Zealand. I didn't mind leaving Australia but was sad that my driving job had come to an end. We docked at Invercargill on the morning of 10th December. To my surprise and delight a local detachment of the New Zealand Army provided us a staff car.

It was driving duties once more, this time in a 1949 Ford V8 flat head sedan painted in drab army green.

We spent an uneventful four days at Invergargill before sailing for exercises with our sister ship HMS Consort and units of the RNZN on our way north.

We tied up outboard of Consort in the city of Auckland on the evening of 23rd December 1956. Danny and I were off duty on Christmas Eve and Christmas Day, and we headed ashore just before noon. Auckland was quiet with few people about. This was probably because it was Christmas Eve. Many businesses were closing or had already closed. We found a small café and decided to stop in for a bite of lunch. Spotting two pretty girls at one of the tables we sat at the table next to them. Before lunch was over the four of us were sitting together.

After lunch we decided to attend a matinee at one of the local cinemas. The girls wanted to see 'Oklahoma' a Rodgers and Hammerstein musical. Not into musicals or love stories, I suggested we go to see 'Battle of the River Plate'. After much discussion the sinking of the Graff Spee won the day.

It was dark when we re-emerged from the cinema. The city had rolled up the sidewalks and gone to bed. We wandered the empty streets devoid of ideas of what to do next.

In a back street we happened upon a brightly lit Italian restaurant. Music blared from within and the place seemed to be crowded. Danny tried the door but it was locked. We were moving on when it burst open and we were invited inside. I never found out if it was a family, the staff, or local Italian club holding the party but we happily joined in.

Around midnight we rolled back onto the street with our girlfriends. We told the girls we had no place to stay except, of course, aboard ship. We went to great lengths to explain how difficult it was to sling a hammock, especially when full of Italian wine. Eventually they said what we'd been hinting at all along. Forget the hammocks and come back to our place.

They shared a room in a private home. Sneaking us in undetected was no easy feat. Outside the front door we removed our shoes and tiptoed up the stairs whispering and giggling. The girls' room was at the back of the house and furnished with two single beds. Still whispering and giggling we undressed in the dark.

Danny said, "Hey its Christmas Eve we better get into bed before Santa arrives."

Our laughter almost gave the game away.

The following morning I was suddenly and roughly shaken awake. Still half asleep and bleary eyed from last night's Chianti, I'm told to get under the bed fast. As I struggled to comply a hand swept my clothes under the bed with me.

I was barely out of sight when the door opened and a cheery voice called out. "Merry Christmas girls. I brought you some tea and toast did you have a good time last night? You must have been out late because we didn't hear you come in."

While she chatted with the girls I was holding my breath hoping not to be discovered. I looked across the floor between the landlady's ankles and saw Danny under the other bed. It took all of my will power not to burst out laughing. Danny was looking at me and making silly facial expressions.

Allowing time for the landlady to return downstairs we quietly emerged from under the beds. The girls were anxious for us to dress and leave. Things looked different in the cold and sober light of dawn. I needed to use the toilet but it wasn't going to happen in the house. We considered ways to escape without discovery. We certainly couldn't leave the same way we'd arrived.

The bedroom window looked out over the back porch and it appeared possible to leave via the window. Hopefully we'd lower ourselves onto the roof then down to the ground without making a noise. It was successful and we made a hasty and undiscovered escape.

While this was the sum total of my Auckland adventures there was one rather funny event taking place aboard ship. We had a messmate known as the Red Devil. He came by the name because he sported a huge red beard. It was something he was very proud of.

He was a relic from an older Navy and a rapidly disappearing breed. A career Able Seaman, he'd been in the Navy for at least twenty years. If he were lucky he'd last until his pension took affect. He never aspired to rise above the rating of Able Seaman. The only badges on his uniform were his three good conduct stripes, and they went up and down almost as often as the ships ensign.

I have no idea of his actual age perhaps forty or so, nor do I recall his real name as everyone called him Red.

Late on Christmas Eve Red staggered aboard and promptly flaked out on a bench. Some of the lads decided to give him a shave. Well, actually half a shave. They shaved the right side of his face clean leaving the left side still bearded. When Red went to the bathroom the next morning he got the shock of his life. With no alternative he removed the rest of his beard and later went ashore again.

That evening he returned in his usual drunken state. He crossed over the Consort and headed for our gangway only to be stopped by the bos'uns mate. Not recognizing him, the bos'uns mate assumed he was a member of Consorts crew. Of course the bos'uns mate of the Consort didn't recognise him either. For a few minutes Red found himself stranded on the gangway between the ships.

Eventually someone realised who he was and allowed him to return aboard.

On the morning of the 27th December we slipped our mooring lines and sailed out into the Pacific. Fiji was our destination for the New Year of 1957.

Chapter 5
The Islands

There are many tiny islands in the Pacific Ocean and I can't remember the names of all those we visited. Fiji was our first port of call after leaving New Zealand. We entered the harbour on the morning of New Year's Eve and tied up near the city of Suva.

No jeeps or cars were provided this time so it was back to regular shipboard routine for me. I was on duty that day and detailed as Shore Patrol for the upcoming evening festivities. It was not a good night to be Shore Patrol as it promised to be one of the busiest nights of the year.

Around 1900hrs we assembled at the Suva Police Headquarters where we were to team up with the local police. Before heading out on patrol we were invited to join our Fijian colleagues in a traditional ritual. Forming a wide circle on the grass we sat with our legs crossed and waited as half a coconut shell containing a mysterious liquid was passed to each one of us in turn. Each person had to drink the contents while everyone clapped. When it reached me I slowly raised it, closed my eyes and swallowed as quickly as possible. It actually tasted quite good with no noticeable or detrimental side effects.

As the New Year was ushered in we were kept busy loading legless shipmates into the police vehicles for transporting back to the ship.

On the 2nd January we sailed off into the Pacific heading for a tiny island under British control. The ship arrived before dark the same day and secured alongside a somewhat unstable jetty. It was too late for shore leave.

The following morning the Skipper was invited to Government House. The Governor wanted to ask for a small favour. On the Captain's return we were informed that we'd be carrying some passengers to a nearby island. As we prepared to leave the harbour our passengers arrived. With them came their worldly goods, children, animals, furnishings and the kitchen sink!

The animals consisted of goats, pigs, chickens and at least two dogs. Some animals were in makeshift cages others were led by children on lengths of rope.

The island was only two hours steaming and as the weather was warm it was decided our passengers and livestock could remain on deck. The trip went without mishap and we soon arrived at our destination.

That was when the Navigator announced the island was completely circled by a coral reef. There was no harbour or a suitable place to unload our guests. It was impossible to use the motor launch or the whaler because they would ground on the reef. The passengers might not have been a problem. The animals, all with a strong aversion to getting wet, definitely were.

The solution was far from perfect but under the circumstances it was the only option. Using a carley-float, two crewmembers paddled ashore. They took ropes and a block and tackle with them. We secured a line from the shore to the ship. This allowed us to pull one carley-float to shore while the other returned to the ship. I should explain what a carley- float is because it was not ideally suited for our purpose. Imagine a large oval shaped cork life ring with rope netting in the center to prevent a body falling through. It is a great rescue raft in the event a ship should sink. However it was never designed to transport pigs, goats or chickens. Especially not chickens.

It was well after midnight when we finally shipped the last of the bits of furniture ashore. It had become necessary to rig searchlights to see what we were doing.

Loading the animals into the rafts had been the most difficult task. Manhandling goats and pigs was bad enough, but chickens were something else. They kept escaping, half flying and half swimming. Their owners screamed at the sailors who laughed and splashed as they tried to retrieve the elusive birds.

We were also aware of an altogether bigger danger and needed to post lookouts for the duration. The South Pacific is a notorious hunting ground for sharks.

It took close to eight hours to complete this madcap operation. Our Skipper was fuming that our schedule was delayed. I imagine he wasn't happy with the less than forthcoming Governor either and his inaccessible island.

We next visited an Australian Naval Base located on another small island. At least this one had a harbour. There was no town where we could spend our shore leave. A naval canteen on the base was the only watering hole. Members of our crew sat on lounge chairs around the pool sipping Australian beer. A few propped up the bar or sat on stools.

Had the Aussies been smarter they would have made no mention of the swimming pool. But at 2100 hours it was announced that the pool was closed. While open no one was interested. Besides, after the recent chickens-in-the-water festival you'd think no one would feel much like swimming. However, now that the pool was closed, well, that was a different matter entirely. Within half a minute the pool was filled with noisy and mostly fully clothed swimmers.

Danny and I sat near the bar quietly sipping our last beers. We knew it would be just a matter of time before the Shore Patrol arrived. We heard the sound of a whistle followed by shouts to vacate the pool immediately. The orders came from a young Sub Lieutenant who had two duty sailors as his back up. No one was listening so the young officer positioned himself at the waters edge shouting and pointing at individuals in the water.

Such a foolish thing to do. With his whistle still blowing he suddenly plunged head first into the deep end. The Shore Patrollers rushed to the side of the pool and instantly joined him in the water. Except for the three officials now struggling in the water the pool had miraculously emptied.

Danny and I got out of there fast in case we were blamed or called as witnesses. As we fled the scene we heard shouts of 'Limey bastards!' and a few other unmentionable names.

The Cockade sailed early the next morning. If the Captain knew we'd out stayed our welcome it was never mentioned.

During the remainder of 1957 we visited Japan and South Korea. We visited Hong Kong on several occasions and patrolled the Strait of Formosa. The latter to show the flag and remind Mainland China we supported the Nationalists on Formosa. Toward the end of the year we returned to Singapore for refit and repair, rest and recreation.

There was considerable unrest in Singapore and on the mainland of Malaya. People were tired of British rule and sought independence. But the biggest fear was the possibility of a communist take over. In French Indo China (later known as Vietnam) the French army was struggling to retain power. The dangerous spread of Communism was a very real fact.

On several occasions I found myself an armed guard on convoy duty. We escorted dockyard workers to and from work. Armed meant carrying a 303 rifle and five rounds of ammo with strict orders not to fire. The order seemed to contradict the purpose of being armed in the first place. The officer in charge rode in a jeep at the head of the convoy. Should someone find it necessary to shoot he first needed permission from the Commander. Fortunately the situation never arose. If it had it meant running to the head of the convoy. Obtain permission to shoot run back to your vehicle and aim at a target that was long gone.

I was later assigned to act as a guard on the trains travelling between Singapore, Kuala Lumpur and Penang. The old coal burning steam engines needed to stop quite often to take on water, and these stops were tense occasions, usually occurring during darkness and deep in the jungle. Bands of Communist guerrillas were known to be roaming around the Malayan jungle and these stops were tailor made for them to launch an ambush.

Standing guard on the open platforms at each end of a carriage was a precarious place to be. We couldn't see anything out in the darkness, yet we were visible to anyone hiding in the dense vegetation. I did several of those guard duties, fortunately all of them without incident.

Christmas of 1957 was celebrated alongside in Singapore, and it was a quiet affair compared with the Auckland adventure of the previous year.

In1958 we returned to patrol the area around Hong Kong. The weather was foul, with rough seas and winds that reached gale force eight. I watched a few of the Chinese junks sailing in this weather and I was amazed at the skill of their seamanship. Most junks were crewed by a whole family, including the grand-parents, young babies and often several animals. Their skill in handling these frail looking craft was impressive, but I definitely would not have changed places with them.

Hong Kong was a marvellous place to visit. The harbour was alive with junks and sampans, and the docks lined with freighters loading and unloading car-go. Crowded and busy ferries constantly cruised back and forth to Kowloon and the Portuguese territory of Macao.

Of the many places I visited during my Naval ca-reer, Hong Kong remains the most fascinating. A city teeming with millions of people from many different walks of life. A person could get just about anything they wanted in any one of the tiny, crowded streets and alleyways. Everything was for sale, watches, chi-na, cameras, radios, tattoos, tailors and girls, and girls, and girls.

The Royal Navy provided two 'Naval Personnel Only' clubs, the China Fleet Club and the Union Jack Club. These were the only places where we could es-cape from the constant pressure of people trying to sell us something.

Nevertheless, we often walked the streets of endless stalls and carts selling souvenirs and trinkets. Many members of the crew came back on board with tattoos. One stoker had no less than fifty-two. His body was covered in a variety of dragons, hearts, ships, dancing girls, and even religious scenes. On his back was a huge tattoo of Jesus steering the ship to safety. His left buttock featured a sentry saying 'Halt, who goes there?' At each elbow was a tattoo of a hinge, under each nipple 'Mild' and 'Bitter'.

I admit to being tempted once or twice but I managed to return home tattoo free. Something I'm quite proud of today. But tattooing was hard to avoid and it was made more difficult by my shipmates constantly claiming that I was scared of the needle.

If I *was* scared of the needle, it was because of the risk of infection. New tattoos would scab over and then required treatment with penicillin. There was no hygiene in the tattoo shops of Hong Kong. Catching a nasty infection from dirty needles was a regular occurrence. The ship's sickbay was often kept busy treating ailing sailors.

A much more widespread problem in the Far East was venereal diseases. It was considered so bad in Japan that the Navy issued contraceptives at the gangway to sailors going ashore.

Of course we thought it was a great laugh to stick pinholes in them before handing them out.

Near the end of the summer of 1958 we were notified that HMS Cockade, an old ship with dated weapons and equipment, was paying off and returning home to Devonport.

Her usefulness had come to an end. The final week in Hong Kong was a busy time. The Skipper purchased an MG sports car and the Engineer bought a Vespa scooter. Stowing these items on board wasn't an easy task. A destroyer is not designed to carry cargo. The car ended up being wrapped in canvas and lashed down aft of 'Y' Gun.

If war was declared on the way home, the car could easily be dropped over the side. A risk more likely than war was running into a force ten gale, then it would probably be washed over the side. The scooter, being considerably smaller, was secured in one of the ships passageways.

During the years on the Far East station, HMS Cockade employed several locals as stewards, cooks and to run the ships laundry. Now that we were heading for home they had to be discharged. This left quite a gap in the service, particularly for the ship's officers. The biggest loss for them was the laundry. Our tropical uniforms were white, and while the crew didn't wear white very often, the officers did. Danny and I saw a great opportunity here and we volunteered to operate the laundry.

Our offer was gladly accepted and we set up in the wardroom head. It was the only place with a bathtub.

Running the laundry had several advantages, and working 9 to 5, was one of the better ones. We took particular care of the Skipper's uniforms as an added security of our employment.

The laundry meant no watch keeping duties for us either. We could turn in at night and not have to rise until the hands were called the next morning.

On the morning we were due to steam for home, a problem arose. The ship was under orders to sail at 0800 hours, and the Red Devil was missing. He was so often in trouble, I think the Skipper would have gladly left him behind.

A member of the crew missing a ship when its about to sail was a serious offence. But missing a ship that was about to sail to the other side of the world was as serious as it could get. Red was heading for a lengthy stay in the brig, if indeed he ever managed to return to England.

The term 'Paying Off' is used when a ship's career is ending. When a ship is leaving its home base it is traditional to hold a closing ceremony. At the masthead we flew our Paying Off pennant, and the ship's company stood to attention along the side of the ship in full dress uniforms.

The jetty was crowded with military dignitaries. The Commander-in-Chief of Hong Kong stood ready to take the salute from his dais. The Royal Marine band was playing Heart Of Oak. We stood smartly at our stations as the ship slowly edged the bow away from the dock. The gangway was removed and only a stern rope remained attached.

It was at this moment that a rickshaw suddenly appeared and raced toward us with the Red Devil frantically urging the runner to greater speed. Red was in a dishevelled state, half in and half out of uniform. In the ensuing commotion all the shore personnel, including the Admiral, turned to look.

Scrambling out of the rickshaw and throwing money at the driver, Red raced for the stern of the ship. Fortunately it was still only a foot or so from the dock. Leaping for his life he half landed, half hit the stern. He was quickly hauled aboard and bundled down the nearest hatch.

It was very difficult for anyone to keep a straight face; though I'm not sure those on the bridge saw the humour in what had just taken place.

And that was my last memory of Hong Kong. It was an amusing, but also a sad ending to so many happy times.

I don't remember what punishment Red received because he was so often under one form of punishment or another.

Chapter 6
Homeward Bound.

As we sailed for home, the course we were taking meant we would visit several new ports along the way. Our estimated time of travel to the UK was approximately four weeks, but much depended on how long we'd have to wait to enter the Suez Canal. The British were quite unpopular in Egypt since the 1956 war. Actually, it was safe to say that we hadn't been popular before the war either.

During my two years on HMS Cockade I'd begun training as a Radar Operator, and I passed the shipboard exams to become an RP3 (u). This stood for Radar Plotter Third Class, the U denoting that I was unqualified. Whichever trade you choose in the Navy you had to go on that specific training course, and this would normally mean being transferred to a shore establishment specializing in that particular trade. The Radar School was at HMS Harrier, an establishment that was located in the South of Wales. I was hoping to go straight there from HMS Cockade.

Our first port of call en-route home was to Ceylon, (Sri Lanka today) which was just a fuelling stop with no shore leave granted. We were only along side for roughly five hours, and then it was back to sea.

Everyone was anxious to get home. Two years was a long time to be away from family and friends. Several of the crew who had married before they were sent out to the Far East was now fathers, and they had never seen or held their sons or daughters.

After leaving Ceylon and sailing around the bottom of India, we headed for the Red Sea. After a brief stop in Aden we steamed towards the Suez Canal. We dropped anchor in the Gulf of Suez and began the long wait for the Egyptians to provide us with a pilot.

We had to wait four days while a variety of merchant ships and tramp steamers were given priority.

During this period we were kept busy with the continuous stream of little boats that came out to us trying to sell their wares. I had already bought all the gifts I needed for the folks back home, yet it was difficult not to be tempted by the variety of items offered.

During the last two years I'd collected a variety of mostly worthless coins from my many ports of call. I wondered if I could use them now to trade with an Arab merchant. As soon as I showed him my bag of coins I got his full attention and the bargaining began. I ended up with a red fez hat and an imitation camel saddle. The saddle was actually a stool for use in the home.

Traveling through the Suez Canal was an interesting, but very slow, experience. The pilot had to watch our ship's wake very closely, because a rough wake would cause a lot of damage to the sandy banks of the canal.

Once we entered the Mediterranean we resumed our course and speed for Malta. Here we tied up alongside an American destroyer. There was always a good-natured rivalry between the British and US Navy, and it was mostly of the humorous sort.

The US vessel had her motto emblazoned on each side of the bridge that said 'Second to None.'

The next morning the signal flags flying from our yardarm read 'None.'

I can't be sure but I expect the Americans did read the flag message, because when we later slipped our lines they piped the ship to attention and saluted us.

The last stop en route to Plymouth was Gibraltar. But only a few lads went ashore we were saving our money for the upcoming leave.

Once alongside in Devonport Dockyard everyone prepared to go on three weeks leave. It was a heady time. The Regulating Office was busy organizing travel warrants, while Customs officials checked us for duty free purchases. No one was actually arrested, though I dare say a few had more than the allowable number of duty free cigarettes.

At the railway station some two hundred sailors jostled to find comfortable seats on the London express. I ended up in the same compartment as the Red Devil. While I heaved my heavy suitcase onto the overhead luggage rack, he hoisted a small barrel of scrumpy (cider) onto the same rack. He proceeded to tap the barrel and, with his own glass, poured himself a pint.

By the time the train began to move he'd already started on his second pint. When we reached London he was in a drunken sleep. I left him with his barrel and headed for the Heysham boat train. That was the last time I ever saw the Red Devil.

Being home again with family and friends was wonderful. I was amazed how much Anna's son John had grown.

It was back to dancing at the Plaza on a Saturday night. Most of my old flames had moved on by then, or were going steady. It wasn't a problem though, because there were lots more girls to go around.

My good friend and mentor Phil Carroll also spent his leave in Belfast. He originally came from Tralee on Ireland's West coast, home of the well-known ballad 'The Rose of Tralee'. He was engaged to a Belfast girl, and a marriage was on a not too distant horizon.

Both Phil and I had long since moved beyond the Catholic-Protestant thing. In the Navy there was no room for such bigotry. However, in Belfast we were aware of the divisions and we had to be careful where we went. That didn't stop me attending his wedding. But the reality of life in Northern Ireland in the fifties and sixties was very sad indeed. My shipmate and fellow laundry worker, Danny Gorman, married a catholic girl from Londonderry. I later heard that neither of the families attended the wedding because it was a mixed marriage.

Three weeks later it was back to Devonport Barracks. I reported to the accommodation office for instructions on my billet. During leave period HMS Cockade had been emptied of men and material, and it was now moored in the creek to await her fate.

I was lodged in a Junior Rates barrack with the rest of our old crew, and my last days as a member of Cockade was among the saddest of my Naval career. During the previous two years I'd made many friends and we'd become like family, but now it was all over.

There were approximately sixty of us in the barrack, and each new posting slowly reduced our numbers. I was hoping and waiting for the word that I was to be posted to the radar school. But it wasn't to be. Instead I was going to a new anti-submarine frigate, HMS Eastbourne. She was presently stationed at

Chatham and was part of the Londonderry squadron. The Eastbourne wore the Ulster symbol of a red hand on each side of her funnel.

I was among the last to receive my orders, and by then the barrack was a quiet and lonely place. My footsteps echoed as I passed between the rows of empty bunks. I was pleased to be stationed close to home, but I was also disappointed not to be selected to the radar school.

On the 21st April 1958, at 0800 hours I departed Plymouth for Chatham to join my new ship. The Eastbourne was a thoroughly modern frigate, far more advanced than the old Cockade. We had much better accommodation, with smaller numbers sharing a mess. Bunks replaced hammocks, and we ate in a cafeteria-style mess hall.

It's difficult to explain my feelings on leaving Cockade. It was almost like joining a different Navy. HMS Cockade was a part of an older wartime Navy of hammocks, portholes and three badge able seamen. To this day I still remember the names of many shipmates from my two years aboard that grand old lady.

Chapter 7
HMS Eastbourne

My time aboard the Eastbourne lasted just over one year. I made a good friend named Teddy Treleaven. He was a young Ordinary Seaman from London but his family was formerly from Ulster.

Compared to HMS Cockade, the Eastbourne had a very young crew and I saw myself as quite an old salt, having traveled around most of the world in the past two years. Few others on board could claim to have visited as many foreign ports as I had.

At nineteen, I was one of the senior ratings in the Seaman's mess. I was assigned radar duties when we were at sea and Quartermaster duties while in harbour. The latter wasn't as grand as the title might suggest. It was merely guard duty on the gangway regulating anyone who wanted to come on board or go ashore.

I was also responsible for piping the ship's routine over the tannoy system (loud speakers) and calling the hands each morning. I admit I took a particular delight in the latter duty.

There were two young National Servicemen in our mess, probably among the last before this compulsory service was ended. One of them was a Jehovah Witness and he took a lot of abuse because of his beliefs. I really felt quite sorry for him. As a Jehovah Witness he was also a pacifist, and this didn't sit well with many of the crew. He was often taunted with the question; 'what would you do if someone started to rape your wife?'

He would answer by saying he'd fight the attacker with words, and this always resulted in more taunting and ridicule. His particular branch of religion didn't impress me much, but I did admire the young sailor's courage and conviction.

We sailed from Chatham to carry out our sea trials, and to train and turn the crew into an efficient team. The trials took several weeks.

One of the big advancements in submarine warfare at the time was the development of a new weapon known as Squid. The old procedure of dropping depth charges off the stern in the hope of hitting a submarine had one major disadvantage. During this kind of operation the ship would lose contact with the target giving it an opportunity to escape.

The Squid was different in that it was still located aft, but the charges were fired high over the bow and dropped well ahead of the ship. This meant that the Sonar operators could maintain contact with the target and make life very difficult for the poor guys down below.

Once the Sea Trials were completed we sailed along the east coast to visit Eastbourne, the seaside town that our ship was named after. We were made very welcome there and in the following days everyone had a ball.

A local cinema was showing a war film about a US destroyer and German U boat called 'The Enemy Below' and we were invited to a private Matinee showing. We spread a rumour to the greenest members of our crew that, as it was a training film, attendance was compulsory.

Then it was back to sea and more training, exercising with German and Swedish Naval vessels in the North Sea and Baltic. At the end of May we returned to Chatham for our summer leave.

Whilst I'd been in the Far East my family moved from Thames Street to a larger and nicer house on Glencairn Street. The new house had a parlour, a living room and a separate kitchen. Upstairs there were two large bedrooms, with a third bedroom in the attic. But the very best feature was the inside toilet and bathtub. We even had hot water. It seemed we were moving up in the world.

A combination of reasons caused us to move. I think the main reason was because of Dan Hughes.

Dan owned a greengrocery on Divis Street. My sister Anna worked for him and over the years he'd become a close friend of our family. He lived a lonely existence in a small flat above his shop. Things might have remained that way but for an unforeseen event. Two of Dan's relatives, parents with a large family, suddenly died. I'm not sure if it was due to an accident or illness, but it resulted in their children being divided up amongst relatives. Dan found himself a parent to a ten-year old boy named Noel.

Seeing how difficult the situation was, Anna suggested they move in with us. It was the ideal solution but not practical in the space available at Thames Street. Hence the reason we moved to a larger home

That summer leave was my first time in the new house. One afternoon while I was returning from town I noticed two young girls sitting on the outside wall of the house next door. I took little notice of them as they were both dressed in school uniforms and obviously quite young.

As I passed by one of the girls said, "Hi Rock."

I was taken by surprise, but I was also quite flattered. In those days Rock Hudson and Doris Day were the popular heartthrobs of the silver screen.

I smiled and continued walking. When the same girl called me by my name, curiosity got the better of me. She was a pretty girl and it occurred to me I could have returned her compliment by calling her Doris. I turned back to ask her how she knew my name.

However, as I stopped and turned, they both jumped off the wall and ran giggling across the street and into a house. At the same moment I spotted Noel and John peeking around the corner with silly grins on their faces. I didn't need to be a detective to figure out how the girls knew my name. In later years, if a girl in the street needed to know my movements, they only had to check with Noel or John. I went indoors, thinking the moment was over and would quickly fade from memory. I was never more wrong. The 'Hi Rock' incident would eventually play a significant part in my future and it would become etched in my memory for the rest of my days.

During my leave a dispute had arisen between the British and Icelandic Governments, and I was about to become directly involved.

Iceland had increased her three-mile territorial waters to twelve miles, and this caused a huge uproar within the British fishing industry. Iceland declared that any foreign trawlers found inside her new territorial boundaries would be arrested and towed into Reykjavik.

To enforce their new territorial waters they employed three gunboats to patrol the area. Britain refused to recognize the new limit and insisted that the British trawlers would continue fishing in their traditional waters. In response to the gunboats, the Royal Navy would provide protection for her trawler fleet.

So at the end of July 1958 we sailed for Iceland, and the beginning of what became known as the Cod Wars! We remained on station for the month of August, patrolling the disputed waters.

The northern most part of Iceland is on the Artic Circle, in the land of the Midnight Sun. The darkness lasted for about two hours, starting around midnight. The same couldn't be said for the fog. It was endless. In such conditions radar becomes a very necessary and vital piece of equipment. The operators needed to be on constant alert. Steaming in dense fog amid dozens of trawlers who were liable to suddenly alter course as they chased the fish was a nervy experience.

One morning in early August I was on radar watch in the usual foggy conditions. A long four-hour watch under these tense conditions could be very exhausting work, especially when the officers on the bridge depend solely on radar. The Royal Navy didn't want to be responsible for sinking one of our own trawlers. We posted lookouts on the bridge wings as well. But visibility was barely a hundred yards.

At around 1000 hrs someone brought me a cup of tea but I set the cup to one side. Things were too hectic to drink with so many active contacts on the screen. I had a radiotelephone link with the bridge and I gave constant updates of ship movements within a two-mile range.

Suddenly a strange voice cut into my com-link. It was a trawler trying to relay a message from another trawler. I was confused at first, wondering how he'd reached me on an in-ship system. He sounded very anxious as he transmitted his message. "Trawler Northampton boarded by gunboat. Crew required immediate assistance."

The message ended with the approximate position.

Apparently the radio operator on the Northampton had barricaded himself in the radio shack and was frantically sending messages for help. I immediately relayed the message to the bridge. The alarm was sounded and the ship came to action stations, and within minutes our speed increased to eighteen knots. No one ever asked, but they must have wondered how the radar office came by the information in the first place.

Racing at speed in thick fog and with trawlers all over the place was a very risky and dangerous situation. I was kept busy searching for the target and I had to watch the screen intently, warning of nearby contacts.

Then at the top of my screen I picked up two contacts close together. They were probably the trawler and gunboat. I reported them, then quickly followed up with an intercept course. Then I prayed that I knew what I was doing.

The motor launch was ready to go with our armed boarding party already on board. The moment the Eastbourne stopped the launch was in the water and on its way to the rescue.

Stuck in the radar office I didn't have any idea what was happening up on deck. And in all the excitement I'd lost track of the time. I was startled when my relief arrived to take over. I rushed out on deck, but it was too late to see what had taken place. The boarding party had returned and the launch was back on the davits. The ship had returned to normal routine. Disappointed I headed back down to the mess for lunch.

It was probably fish again. Since arriving on station the trawlers had showered us with a daily supply of fresh fish in gratitude for our protection.

Over lunch I learned what had taken place and I was a bit surprised to hear that no action was required in rescuing the trawler. The moment we appeared the gunboat 'Thor' steamed away leaving her boarding party behind. We hailed them only to be ignored, and we were left holding eight prisoners.

The prisoners seemed friendly enough and not overly upset at being abandoned by their shipmates. Nevertheless, they were the enemy and had to be treated as such. The Eastbourne didn't have a brig large enough for eight people. I'm not sure if we had a brig at all. A lower mess deck was vacated and the prisoners were accommodated there with an armed guard at the hatch. Our displaced crew had to doubled up in other messes.

The ship provided the prisoners with fresh clothing, food, cigarettes and a can of beer per day. While they didn't appear threatening, the guards had to remain vigilant. They were escorted at all times for meals, exercise and washing etc. Sabotage was a real possibility. If the ship was damaged or disabled in any way, we were a very long way from home, and it was unlikely we'd find any help locally.

The question of what to do with our prisoners arose as the end of the patrol approached. I wasn't privy to any negotiations between the Captain and the Admiralty, but speculation on the mess deck was that the government wouldn't want us returning to England with eight Icelandic prisoners. It was easy to imagine the sort of field day the news media would have. I could see them hovering around the docks, scrambling to interview any sailors they could catch. And God only knows what nonsense some of our lads would have told them.

However, a simple solution was found and the decision made. On the last night of our patrol, and in the brief hours of darkness, we rigged false lights to disguise ourselves as a merchant ship. Then we sailed as near as we dared to the entrance to Reykjavik Harbour, lowered the ship's whaler with the prisoners aboard and told them to row for shore.

The sun was rising as Iceland disappeared over the horizon and we headed for home, less one Admiralty-issued whaler. Many years later I heard that our whaler was on display in the Reykjavik Maritime Museum.

We spent a week in Chatham, taking on fuel and re-stocking with supplies. That included the issue of a new whaler. Then we sailed across the North Sea to the Norwegian fjords, visiting Norway, Denmark and Sweden.

October found us in Scapa Flow where we joined others ships of the Home Fleet to prepare for exercises north of the Faeroe and Shetland Islands, waters where we'd be guaranteed the very foulest of weather.

On completion of the exercises we returned to Londonderry. I managed to hitch hike home for the weekend. I was saving to buy a car and I didn't want to waste money on bus or train fares. I hitched back to Londonderry from Belfast on the Sunday afternoon.

We returned to Chatham in December for a short refit, and to allow the ships company to take leave for the Christmas holidays. I didn't buy a car as planned, because something more interesting presented itself. It was a BSA Golden Flash motorcycle with a sidecar.

This was the 650cc twin 1952 model and I could hardly wait to get it out on the road. I'd never ridden a motorcycle before, and certainly not one with a sidecar. I gave myself a few unpleasant surprises on my first few attempts. Like making a left hand turn without due care and causing the sidecar to leave the ground, which nearly upset the bike.

On another occasion I badly scared a shipmate who was riding in the sidecar. He was frantically trying to get my attention because the sidecar wheel was on the sidewalk, and I was missing lampposts, fire hydrants and people by inches.

Over the next few days my riding abilities improved. Fortunately I didn't kill myself, or anyone else. When I went home on Christmas leave, I left the bike on the jetty beside the ship covered with canvas and guarded by whoever was on duty at the gangway.

When I returned from leave a few days before the New Year of 1959, a draft notice was waiting for me. At last! I was going to HMS Harrier to begin an RP3 radar course.

On the eleventh of January 1959, with my sidecar loaded and me decked out in army surplus goggles, helmet and waterproof coat, I hit the road for Wales.

Chapter 8
Radar & Wrens

Setting out on a long motorcycle journey in the month of January required a lot more thought than I'd given it. January is better described as the dead of winter. I left Chatham Dockyard at 0800 hours on 12th January 1959 clad in Army surplus motorcycle clothing better suited to desert warfare than a winter crossing of England.

Nevertheless that's exactly what I did, leaving on a cold and wet morning. Three days before my twentieth birthday, I faced a daunting three hundred miles of slow winding roads passing through endless towns and villages. There were no fast two-lane highways in those days, and the speed limits varied from 30mph to 50mph,which was the maximum. Numbers of buses and lorries used the roads and getting stuck behind one could last for miles. Using a map while riding a motorcycle in the rain was impossible without pulling over. Around 10.30 am I passed through Croydon and Reading having covered perhaps fifty miles. Rain was seeping through my clothing. I was cold and wet as I pressed on to Newbury. I stopped at pub called the Spotted Bovine. I ordered a pint of best bitter and a pork- pie and sat beside a glowing fire. Leaving the pub half an hour later the rain had stopped. The improving weather lifted my spirits a little.

An hour later it was snowing. It was a mixture of rain and sleet that made the roads treacherous and slowed traffic. Late afternoon I crossed the Bristol Channel and entered Wales.

Here the roads quickly became even more winding and narrow. Just west of Newport, exhausted, half frozen and starving I pulled into a bed and breakfast for the night.

The next morning I was up and on the road very early. I felt refreshed and eager to reach my destination that afternoon. The bad weather continued with cold temperatures and more sleet. As I travelled deeper into Wales the roads became narrow lanes with high hedgerows on both sides. Often so narrow it was impossible to pass an oncoming vehicle.

About a mile apart were widened areas where one vehicle could pull over while another passed. It seemed the rule was the vehicle nearest the passing area would back up. In a car this works quite well as cars have a reverse gear. Motorcycles don't. I'd have to stop and push the bike back.

At three o'clock that afternoon I had arrived in the town of Haverfordwest. I was filthy and tired but a mere fifteen miles from the base. I asked a local policeman for directions. Impressed, he listened to my adventures while pointing me in the direction of Harrier. When finally the main gate of HMS Harrier came into view it was a wonderful sight. I reported to the guardhouse and received my instructions. I found my barrack, had a hot bath and collapsed on my bunk.

HMS Harrier began in1947 as an extension to the naval air station at Dale, HMS Goldcrest. It was first known as Goldcrest 2. It was used as a test centre for new radar and meteorology equipment.

In 1948 it became HMS Harrier, and radar training began with the arrival of the first classes. The camp consisted of mostly portable buildings, prefabricated accommodations, Nissan huts and such. The largest building was the Cotton Trainer, a place where I'd spend much of my time while learning the radar trade. Harrier closed down in 1960 and radar training moved to HMS Dryad in Southwick

During my first days at Harrier I was re-united with several of my old Ganges shipmates. In particular I remembered Michael Foster and Andy Brown, classmates from the Ganges Annex.

The radar plot course covered a period of six months. I found the training familiar having done much of the same thing aboard ship for the last two years. Memorizing the sequence for turning on several different types of radar sets wasn't so easy. A unit might consist of three or four large cabinets containing radio valves and tubes. They took time to warm up before they were operational. Turning the wrong switch or using a wrong sequence could result in burning out a circuit. This was guaranteed to bring the wrath of an instructor down upon your head. I learned that in many areas of training we worked closely with radar-qualified Wrens. The term 'wren' was substituted for WRNS—Woman's Royal Naval Service. Harrier had a compliment of some eighty Wrens, most of whom were in the radar branch. To say that eighty Wrens could be a distraction would have been an understatement. Aboard ship we had long since become used to the absence of female company. At Harrier we might bump into a wren at every turn. Of course there was absolutely nothing wrong with that. It was a simply marvellous situation, just like living in paradise. The wrens usually found themselves on the receiving end of most jokes taking place at the camp. The first thing a shipmate asked me was, did I know the difference between a wren and a sailor? I replied, "I'm sure you are going tell me". Well it's obvious a wren wears a double-breasted jacket. Waiting one morning for our instructor to arrive some fool decided to give us his slant on algebra. On the backboard he wrote the following example (AB/wren = wren/due = AB/C's) For those of you not sailors let me explain. We were all AB's (Able Seaman) and wren over due meant she was pregnant, the responsible AB then volunteered to go overseas. Another regular event was to wake up and see a variety of wren's underwear flying from the masthead. Embarrassing for the owners whose names were clearly stamped on each item. The morning colour party took pleasure in attempting to return the items after hoisting the Ensign. Needless to say, no wren ever asked to have her missing knickers returned.

In my six months at Harrier I saw romances blossom and wither among my shipmates

Owning a motorcycle and sidecar proved to be a valuable asset. Indeed any vehicle was an asset when so far from the nearest town. Within my first week at Harrier I was dating a very pretty wren name Margaret. She was one of the few wrens not in the radar branch. Margaret wore a trade badge of crossed flags denoting the Signals Branch. Better known in the Navy as a bunting tosser.

We quickly became very close and we spent every available off-duty moment together. We divided our time together between the base cinema, Haverfordwest and long walks along the cliff pathways. Our romance grew steadily and for the first time in my life I was truly in love. In previous romances I'd often *thought* I was in love. However this time it just felt right and had to be the real thing. Anyone seeing me heading to the barracks after kissing Margaret goodnight would probably have agreed. I literally bounced back to the mess leaping in the air to kick my heels together. Boy! I must have had it bad.

In Haverfordwest we'd eat supper at a little café on the main street. I usually had sausage and chips while Margaret ordered mushrooms on toast. I confess I'd never tasted a mushroom, they reminded me too much of 'shit on a raft'.

In mid March, with the first signs of spring in the air Easter leave began. I wasn't excited to be going home. Leave meant separation from Margaret for two long weeks.

I made the best of it riding my bike home via the Holyhead ferry. In Belfast I visited relatives and friends showing off my machine. One evening I dropped in at McWater's Bakery to pick up my father. I thought he'd be pleased as I lowered him into the sidecar. Especially as I had him home fifteen minutes earlier than usual. He appeared relieved as he climbed out of the sidecar and disappeared indoors. Later he said to Anna "tell that wee fella not to pick me up in that contraption again."

Eventually leave ended and excitedly I returned to Harrier. Margaret and I were reunited and all was well with the world. A few weeks later Margaret invited me to her home in Worcestershire. It was a big step and I was quit anxious about meeting her parents for the first time. What would they think of me? Nevertheless I set about cleaning and polishing the motorcycle for the trip. I hoped my bike would be impressive even if I wasn't.

A few days before we were due to leave a crisis arose. Margaret's parents wrote pleading with her not to travel home on a motorcycle. Her mother considered it much too dangerous. It seemed that just like my father she saw my contraption as unsafe.

Without transportation it looked like the weekend was off. Travelling to Worcestershire in private transportation was difficult enough. Public transportation such as trains and buses were either unavailable indirect or too slow. I scrambled around the camp looking for an alternative. I offered my bike in trade for a car for the weekend. A classmate agreed to swap his 1938 Hillman Minx convertible for my bike. This solved my immediate problem but his car left a lot to be desired. The many faults included a leaky top, worn steering, bald tires and almost non-existent brakes. The only saving grace was the fact that it couldn't reach much over thirty miles per hour. That at least made the need for braking a little less urgent. If Margaret's mother had been aware of these facts my motorcycle might have regained favour.

Spending a whole weekend with Margaret would be wonderful. Upon our arrival in Worcestershire I soon realised I was not favoured as a suitor by her mother. During the weekend we drove to Bristol to visit my brother Tommy and his wife Joan. Tommy had a 1936 Hillman Minx saloon for sale that piqued my interest. I decide to sell the motorbike when I returned to base and buy the car. It was two years older than the borrowed convertible but was in much better condition with brakes that actually worked. Margaret and I arrived back at Harrier late on the Sunday night to a silent and sleeping camp. We unloaded the car, kissed goodnight and returned to our respective messes.

The next morning I returned the ignition key to its owner. He looked a little sheepish when he saw me, and I understood why when I saw my bike tucked in beside our mess block. The sidecar body was sitting on the ground behind it.

Apparently driving down to the village pub with two passengers, one in the sidecar and one on the pillion they hit a bump. The sidecar body parted from the frame and came to an abrupt halt in the middle of the road.

The sudden loss of weight caused the bike to veer off into a hedgerow dumping the two riders in dense thicket. The helpless sidecar passenger was trapped and sitting in the middle of the road. The canopy could only be opened from the outside. No real damage had been done and after thinking about it, it was really quite funny. The bolts holding the sidecar to the frame had rusted and worked loose. I'd never sat in the sidecar so was unaware that a problem existed. However I was most grateful it hadn't happened to Margaret while visiting her parents

I didn't bother repairing the sidecar and removed the frame and wheel from the bike. I placed a 'for sale' ad on the mess hall notice board. A few messmates showed immediate interest and by the end of the second week a deal was concluded and the bike was gone. My next off duty weekend I made tracks to Bristol and bought my brother's Hillman.

In May the radar course became more complicated and we spent a lot of time in the Cotton Trainer learning aerial radar tactics. No one in the class had served aboard an aircraft carrier so the type of radar we now worked with was new and unfamiliar. We surely caused our instructors no end of problems as we attempted to vector aircraft onto enemy targets.

Our aircraft were known as 'Friendly' and we were supposed to guide then to the enemy aircraft, known as 'Bogeys'. It was easy to get confused and mistake a classmate's Friendly as a Bogey. We often ended up shooting down our own planes. Slowly we began to learn and were able to accurately guide a friendly fighter onto a Bogey.

The training was a simulation without real aircraft. I had no desire to do it for real and lived in fear of being posted to an aircraft carrier.

The month of May was a difficult month in more ways than one. I received a letter from home saying Pop was unwell and had to leave work. There was no mention of what was actually wrong with him. The omission caused me concern. I knew Pop never missed work. Whatever was wrong with him must be serious.

Later Anna wrote to explain that he had a large sore on the inside of his mouth. Apparently it was caused by poorly fitting false teeth. I relaxed, thinking it would soon heal and with new better fitting teeth everything would be okay.

The next bad news arrived a few days later. Margaret had received a draft notice to leave Harrier on the 20th June. Her new posting was HMS Mercury the Naval Signal Station located near Portsmouth. I was unprepared for the possibility that Margaret might move. Deep down we both knew it was bound to happen but had chosen not to think about it. I knew when the course ended I'd be drafted and possibly stationed overseas.

The weekend before Margaret was due to leave we packed the Hillman with her many belongings and headed for Worcestershire. She had an unusual collection of items that included a teddy bear named 'Twurly' and a potted cactus called
'Alfred'.

She held Alfred on her lap for the duration of the journey. He actually turned out very handy because during the trip we ran into heavy rain. The Hillman was a saloon car with the centre roof section made of fabric. Over the years the material had deteriorated and rain dripped directly above Margaret's lap. Alfred had never before been so well watered.

After Margaret departed Harrier I suffered indescribable pain and heartache.

I had never before missed someone so completely. We wrote to each other every day and, while it was a thrill to receive letters they only offered small consolation.

The commencement of exams forced me to clear my mind and prepare for the tests ahead. The exams lasted for a whole week and consisted of written, oral and practical. The last thing I wanted to do was fail.

Fortunately I passed, and on the 15th July 1959 I was sewing my newly qualified radar badge on the right arm of my uniform.

In the following days draft notices began to arrive. This could be exciting or disastrous depending on where one was posted.

When my name appeared I was dumbfounded to read I was posted to HMS

Dolphin, to begin submarine training. I didn't recall volunteering for the submarine service. I checked with my Divisional Petty Officer. He looked up my records and sure enough I had put my name forward whilst aboard the

Eastbourne.

Slowly it all came back to me. I remembered that particular tot time when I decided an extra shilling a day was a good idea. Once recovered from the initial shock it really wasn't so bad. The extra pay would certainly be handy. Better still Dolphin was in Portsmouth, and so was Margaret.

I loaded the Hillman with my kit and hit the road. Leaving Harrier my journey would be more comfortable than my January arrival on the motorcycle.

Chapter 9
Submarine Training

HMS Dolphin is located on the Gosport side of the narrow harbour entrance directly opposite old Portsmouth. The drive down was uneventful, the car purred along beautifully. I arrived at the main gate in the early afternoon of July 20th 1959. My base joining routine moved along fast and by suppertime I was settled in my new accommodation. Never before had I been billeted in such palatial quarters. I shared a spacious room with three classmates, and furniture consisting of four bunks, four lockers and a couple of wardrobes.

Wolfe Block, a new building would be my home for the next three months while I completed basic submarine training. This initial training gave us an understanding of the various systems and how they worked. It was similar to taking a crash course in plumbing although some items even plumbers would not encounter. In particular, the very complicated head (toilet) system found on 'T' class boats.

It was the most complicated, and fearful piece of equipment I ever had to deal with. When the instructor explained how to operate it, everyone hoped they would be sent to a different type of boat.

The 'T' class head wasn't flushed in the normal way. The user had to blow its contents to sea. When submerged the sea pressure outside the hull is much greater than inside. Therefore, before blowing the contents of the bowl it was important to consider depth and sea pressure. If the system was charged at a greater air pressure than outside everything worked fine. However, miscalculate depth or pressure and everything sprayed back onto the fool operating the head. The instructor explained it like this, "do it wrong and you'll have freckles for life".

On weekends and off duty days I drove out to Soberton Towers, the Wren's quarters located just beyond Southwick. Margaret and I drove around the beautiful Hampshire countryside. We visited the New Forest stopping at quaint country pubs for lunch or supper. The 'Bold Forester' near the Towers became a favourite spot. Often we sat in the garden sipping lager and lime.

While everything seemed right with my world, things were not so good at home. My father was not recovering. I learned he had a terminal form of cancer and doctors estimated he perhaps had a year to live. A family reunion was planned for August. Jim and his wife Faye would come home from Canada. Tommy and Joan would travel over from Bristol. I was to try and arrange my leave for the same time if possible.

I invited Margaret to spend her summer leave with me in Belfast. I was sure her parents wouldn't agree. As it turned out I was wrong. Perhaps the agreement was influenced because of my father's failing health. Regardless of the reason, I arrived home in late August with Margaret at my side.

Our time in Belfast, with the exception of the sad reason for being there, was quite wonderful. Margaret and I toured the countryside visiting the Mountains of Mourne and the Hills of Donegal.

With Jim and Faye we drove down to Dublin visiting that grand old city's historic places of interest. The car we borrowed for the trip was a 1952 Ford Prefect. Jim being the eldest elected himself the driver. We experienced a few tense moments on the trip because he was unfamiliar with driving on the right. Nor was he very adept at handling the little four-cylinder car with its unpredictable mechanical brakes.

On the return trip to Belfast we had a flat tire. It surely convinced Jim the car was out to get him. Had I not been there to change the wheel we may well have had to walk home.

Saying goodbye to everyone, and in particular my father, at the end of my leave was a very emotional time. I tried not to think about the reason that would bring us together again.

Shortly after returning to duty at the end of August two things happened.

One was bad and the other rather stupid. The bad news was that Margaret was transferred to London. It wasn't a total disaster London was still within reach at weekends. The trusty Hillman would be an ideal means of transport to the capital.

That's when I did the stupid thing. A classmate owned a beautiful 1937 Jaguar 1.1/2 Litre saloon, and offered to trade for the Hillman.

It should have been obvious that no one would trade a Jaguar for a lowly Hillman.

Not unless it had some serious problems. Which of course it did. I was in awe of the impressive chrome grille and huge Lucas headlights and an interior of wood and leather.

I simply couldn't wait to do the swap. I spent the rest of the week polishing and cleaning this fabulous machine. On Friday, with three classmates on board, I guided the Jag through Dolphin's main gate and headed for London. I felt like a king in this wonderful car, and I paid little attention to the steady knock emitting from the engine bay.

I phoned Margaret to say I was coming up driving the marvellous Jag. Just outside of Guilford the steady knock suddenly became an awful clatter. I pulled into the first garage we came across. The mechanic listened for less than a second before declaring the engine had had it. The main bearings were shot and it would be impossible to drive on. He directed me to a scrap yard at the end of the street. The owner there would probably buy the car for parts.

I nursed the ailing Jag into a yard full of derelict automobiles. The grubby looking owner glanced at my car and said, "Eight quid, mate. Best I can do."

I had no choice, the car wasn't going anywhere and I couldn't afford the repairs. Taking the money we grabbed a taxi to the nearest rail station. I eventually arrived in London, and once reunited with Margaret the memory of the disastrous Jag quickly faded.

A few weeks after the Jag incident I received more bad news. Margaret was posted to a Naval Air Station at Lossiemouth, in the North of Scotland. If she'd been posted to the moon it couldn't have been any worse. It was too far north and too expensive to contemplate weekend travel. In fact it would take the best part of a weekend just to get there and back. There was nothing to do. We were in the Navy and went where they sent us. At the end of September we had another of our many teary farewells. I waved as

Margaret boarded the night train to the moon. For the foreseeable future it was back to writing letters.

Back in Dolphin, classroom training continued, with a growing fear of the escape-tank drawing ever closer. The fact that our classroom stood in the shadow of the escape tower didn't help.

Like all things Naval we heard story after story of dreadful happenings during escape training. They were guaranteed we'd be terrified by the time our turn arrived to enter the tank. The stories were of course greatly exaggerated. However, that didn't alter the facts escape training was indeed quite dangerous.

We first had to establish that we were capable of withstanding the pressure at a hundred feet. To confirm this we sat in a recompression chamber, a large round cylinder with a heavy steel door and two portholes. Once the door was sealed, air was vented into the chamber gradually increasing pressure on the occupants. It was critical to keep equalizing the pressure inside our eardrums by pinching nostrils and blowing.

If anyone fell behind he was to raise his hand and the air pressure was reduced until the person cleared his ears. This happened several times and we had to endure the stop start conditions it created. Once everyone was confirmed fit to continue it was off to change rooms. Here we dressed in swimming trunks and travelled to the top of the tank.

Escape training began at the top of the tank, and gradually we worked our way deeper. The first test was to lower oneself into the water, take a deep breath, let go and sink. People who are buoyant will sink somewhere near fifteen feet and then rise back to the surface. Those known as negatively buoyant would keep going down, and had to be brought back to the surface by an instructor.

It was important to know this because escaping from a submarine was by free ascent. In other words the compressed air in our lungs made us buoyant without the need of a life jacket. Inflating a life jacket under pressure would cause it to burst before reaching the surface. The same would happen to our lungs if we didn't continually breath out during our ascent.

The first day of training consisted of the recompression chamber and buoyancy tests. The second day we made ascents from the thirty-foot mark. At the thirty and sixty-foot depths there was a side entrance know as a blister. It was an air/water lock. Once inside the blister and breathing compressed air I had to take a deep breath duck under water and out through the hatch blowing to the surface. Blowing air during the ascent was vitally important and similar to whistling. While in the water we were closely monitored by our instructors. If they spotted someone holding their breath the individual received a punch in the stomach that was guaranteed to restart exhaling.

The thirty-foot ascent was not too difficult and our class completed this phase without difficulty. However, the deeper blister at sixty feet did cause us a little apprehension and concern. I took in as much air as possible before entering the water. With sixty feet of water above me I worried about running out of air. Everything went well and everyone qualified the sixty-foot ascent.

The third day a line of frightened sailors waited outside the 100ft escape compartment which was directly under the tower. Once inside the escape chamber we stood nervously in two rows. The instructor pointed out the various pieces of equipment needed for the escape. The ominous escape hatch through which we would shortly pass loomed silently overhead. For the moment it remained firmly shut.

The compartment was designed exactly like the escape compartment on an actual submarine. The hatch we had entered through was still open giving us a modicum of reassurance. While it remained open it offered a chance to flee. Hanging in front of us in two rows was a mouthpiece connected to an overhead airline. It was explained that once flooding began we must use this equipment to breath. The units were known as BIBS (built in breathing system).

At the centre of the compartment, around the escape hatch, a circular canvas trunk was drawn down to waist level and secured to the deck by four lanyards.

The instructor explained that the compartment would flood to roughly chest height before the pressure equalized inside the chamber. It would be impossible to open the hatch until the inside and outside pressures were the same. Once equalized the escape hatch could be cracked open, allowing water to flood into the canvas trunk. The hatch could then be fully opened and the escapes could begin.

Only silence answered his next question. Did everyone understand and were we ready?

Maybe to give us an extra jolt, he added that once the flooding began it couldn't be stopped, there was only one way out.

It was zero hour. The hatch slammed shut, BIBS were clenched between our teeth, and everyone prepared to start clearing eardrums as the air pressure increased. The flood wheel was spun open and water flooded in. It crept slowly over our feet and ankles, knees and waists.

I was furiously blowing to keep my ears drums ahead of the pressure. When the water reached my chest the pressure equalized. The instructor disappeared into the trunk to crack the hatch. When he reappeared he signalled for the first man to go. As we moved we changed BIBS. When my turn came I was still able to move my limbs but inside I was paralysed with fear. I drew in the largest breath of my life thinking it might be my last.

I ducked under the trunk, straightened my body with my arms at my side and cleared the hatch. Once outside, I concentrated on blowing out air as I rose rapidly toward the distant surface. It was an amazing experience. The tank was brightly illuminated and the water was clear. I was able to read depth markings on the side of the tank as I hurtled upwards. In the span of twenty seconds I was on the surface being told to get out fast before the next man arrived.

There was one other method of escape to learn, the two-man chamber.

Submarines have two escape compartments located fore and aft. Usually there is a two-man chamber in the control room at the centre of the boat. When carrying out the two-man escape we depend on each other's actions. Once inside the chamber and breathing through the BIB system the flood valve is opened. When the pressure equalizes, the hatch can be cracked open. This instantly floods the chamber. The first time it flooded so rapidly it took me by surprise. I was suddenly buoyant and shot upward, banging my head on the hatch. Fortunately there was only fifteen feet of water above the chamber. On my first attempt I tried leaving with the BIBS still in my mouth and managed to fill my lungs with air and water. The high-pressure bubbles in the chamber reduced visibility to almost zero. Still below me was an anxious shipmate who was also trying to get through the hatch.

Instructors saw what happened and when we finally spluttered to the surface we were promptly sent back to do it again. The second time, now well prepared for what was to come, we executed a very professional escape.

The escape training was the biggest hurdle that we had to overcome during the course and we all successfully passed. Only a few written and oral exams remained and once completed we would be posted to operational boats.

On the 15th October 1959, with the course completed, I was posted to the submarine Amphion, refitting in Portsmouth Dockyard.

It was a proud moment, exchanging my HMS Dolphin cap tally for HM/SM Submarines. In the Submarine Service everyone wore the same cap tally and our motto was 'We Come Unseen'. However, if you've ever been on board an old diesel-electric boat you will understand why we altered the motto to 'We Come Unclean'.

There was a submarine badge available but no professional submariner ever wore it. It resembled a sausage on a stick rather than a submarine. After I left the service a much nicer new metal badge was issued designed with two facing dolphins with a crown and anchor at the centre. The badge was trimmed in gold and worn above medal ribbons on the left. It was certainly a more worthy symbol to denote members of the Silent Service.

While the Amphion was undergoing a major refit in the dockyard the crewmembers had to live ashore. We were paid a living allowance and given a list of addresses of homes where we could find room and board. I moved into a house at 37 Harley Street in the Fratton district. It was within walking distance of the dockyard.

Ted and Edna Perry were great people and during my stay they made me feel like one of the family. They had two young daughters, Linda and Karen, and a lovable old dog named Boodie.

Ted was a very knowledgeable car enthusiast whom I wished I'd met while I still had the Jag. A local pub 'The Fitzroy Arms' was an a mere hundred paces from our front door. I spent many evenings leaning on the piano singing along with a pint of best bitter in hand.

On other occasions I played darts, a game that I was never particularly adept at. Ted always seemed to be working on a string of interesting cars in the evenings and weekends. Probably because of his influence, I bought and sold a number of cars myself. Some of them actually ran, many didn't.

One notable vehicle was a 1934 BSA Scout. It was a very strange front wheel drive sports car. Among the items missing from the car was it's convertible top and any noticeable engine compression. Nevertheless I drove it to and from the dockyard for the next few weeks.

It developed an annoying squeak in the front right wheel. I regularly poured oil on the hub and the squeak disappeared. It only lasted for a mile or two before the squeak returned. I finally sold it to a shipmate who claimed he was going to fix the squeak. A few weeks later, as he braked for a school crossing the car stopped and the squeaky wheel kept going.

Margaret and I continued writing to each other every day. What we found to write about and fill three or four pages with is a complete mystery now. But I suppose, when in love as we were and letters our only means of communication, there was always so much to say.

In early November I received a letter from Margaret containing wonderful news. She announced she was coming to Portsmouth on an extended weekend. I was over the moon waiting on the platform as her train pulled into the station.

It was a most marvellous weekend that was over in the blink of an eye. In what seemed like no time I was back on that same platform bidding a teary farewell.

Christmas leave came and went. I went back to Belfast and Margaret to Worcestershire. It was impossible to arrange taking our leave together. I would have gone to Worcestershire in a flash, but without an invitation from her parents it wasn't going to happen.

It was back to Portsmouth in January 1960, as the boat was nearing the end of the refit. We would soon be heading to Scotland for sea trials. I expected the trials would last for approximately six weeks and our home base would be Faslane. I'd given no thought to the fact that on completion of trials the boat was going to Halifax, Nova Scotia. We were to take up duties as part of the 6th Canadian Submarine Squadron.

While I was still in Portsmouth I decided to treat myself to a twenty-first birthday present. I made arrangements to meet Margaret in Edinburgh for a weekend. I arrived at a very early six o'clock on a cold and wet Saturday morning. It had been a long arduous over-night journey and I'd had to use one of my three yearly travel warrants. With Christmas just over I lacked the cash to afford the rail fare and still have money for the weekend.

In Edinburgh I had to wait until noon for Margaret's train to arrive from Lossiemouth. Once she arrived we spent a wonderful, if very brief weekend together. I had to leave early on the Sunday morning in order to be back on time. Poor Margaret had to spend the day in Edinburgh because her train didn't leave until the early hours of Monday morning. I had to face the same long train journey back to Portsmouth. This short weekend visit would be the last real opportunity for us to spend time together.

I arrived back in Portsmouth weary and grubby after spending the greater part of three days aboard a train. I was depressed thinking about my upcoming departure for Canada. This was a two-year commission, stationed on Canada's East Coast. If I'd thought of Lossiemouth as being on the moon, then Canada was surely on Mars. I wouldn't see Margaret for two years. Where she might be stationed by then was anyone's guess.

A solution to my dilemma came from a most unlikely source. On break one morning in January I was in the dockyard canteen. I was reading the Daily Mirror and sipping a cup of tea. A Canadian Submariner whom we knew as Frenchy pulled up a chair and sat down beside me. In those days the RCN were training their personnel in RN boats. They would later buy three British built 'O' class submarines.

"I hear you're an RP3 on the Amphion. I'm the same on the Taciturn," he said with a smile.

I wasn't sure if he was asking a question or just making conversation.

"Are you interested in doing a swap draft? I just got married and I want to go back to Canada with my new bride."

My ears immediately picked up, this could be a way to remain closer to home and Margaret. Taciturn was refitting in the dockyard and was a few months behind us. On completion she was due to join the First Submarine Squadron at Dolphin. I agreed, and in the following days we became close friends filling in the necessary transfer forms. It was usually possible to arrange a swap draft if both commanding officers agreed. In this case there were no objections and on the 4th February I joined the Taciturn.

Too late, I recalled my Dolphin training and the terrifying operation of the head aboard a 'T' class boat.

Chapter 10
Diving Stations

Amphion sailed shortly after my transfer to the Taciturn and I remained an untested submariner having yet to dive underwater. Near the end of February Margaret was transferred to HMS Dauntless a base near Reading. Here she began embarkation preparations for Malta. The Navy seemed set to keep us apart. Margaret would be stationed in Malta for the next two years. I found time for only one brief visit to Reading before her departure. Even though there was no hope of weekend leave I still explored all the possibilities. Military aircraft flew to and from Malta regularly. I inquired into the possibility of hitching a ride during my two-week leave. It was possible, but I had to have enough cash for a return civilian flight should the military one be cancelled. I had no chance of raising enough money in the time available. So my Malta plan never got off the ground so to speak. For now it was back to writing letters every day.

At the end of May the Taciturn completed her refit and we headed out to do our sea trials in and around the lochs of Scotland.

The first dive after a refit is very tense there always exists the possibility that somebody forgot to tighten a bolt or set a valve correctly. The Captain takes the boat slowly deeper while everyone watches and listens for problems. Every creak and groan seems to echo throughout the boat setting nerves on edge.

The silence is sometimes broken when a compartment reports a problem over the intercom. Stern compartment reporting leak at escape hatch flange or some similar defect.

Once these items are corrected we continued to go deeper to reach and test our maximum depth. Occasionally a boat has to return to port to repair the more serious problems. Thankfully the Taciturn was a sound boat reaching its maximum depth and returning safely to the surface to continue our trials.

Having finally dived beneath the waves I saw myself as a submariner. Even the complicated blowing of the head lost its fear.

However it would remain the low point of serving on a 'T' class boat. There was nothing worse than going to the head to find the bowl full to the brim. No one bothered to empty it until it was an absolute necessity. It usually occurred at night when one was half asleep and late for the watch change.

Margaret and I continued writing but I was becoming aware that the period between her letters was lengthening. I decided to do what I should have done before she left for Malta. I purchased an engagement ring and along with a letter proposing marriage I sent it off.

At the same time I wrote to her parents asking for permission to marry their daughter. Two weeks later disaster struck. First, her parents wrote saying they had only allowed Margaret to join the WRNS to further her career. They made no mention of my marriage proposal, but their message was clear. This news alone didn't deter me, we were both over twenty-one and could make our own decisions.

But the second letter really took the wind out of my sails. Margaret wrote to say she was returning the ring because of the customs duty required. Apparently the Maltese customs were charging a duty of £12 sterling.

At this point there was nothing more I could do. A few days later the ring arrived in the mail. Margaret hadn't actually turned down my proposal but more importantly she hadn't said yes either. It was a serious set back that I could do little about. We continued writing to each other but the period between letters continued to lengthen. I refused to believe I was losing Margaret, yet somehow deep down I knew the truth. I don't know when I actually accepted that it was over it just simply seemed to fade away. I was heartbroken, and tried I to handle my depression by drinking too much.

Having an unused engagement ring can be a problem especially when the owner is often drunk. I got engaged at least once during an all-night pub-crawl. What finally happened to the ring, and where it eventually ended up is open to speculation. My shipmates retrieved it once and saved me from doing something stupid. I think in the end I might have dispatched it to the bottom of Portsmouth Harbour. On the other hand perhaps a faded Rose is still awaiting my return to Portsmouth.

Toward the end of the sea trials I made what, at the time, seemed to be a completely harmless decision, but it would eventually have a disastrous effect upon my future.

Coming alongside in Faslane for weekend leave, Matt Smalley, the boat's chef, asked me for a favour.

He planned to rent a car but had no licence, so he asked me if I would drive for him. He wanted to visit his girlfriend and their two-year old daughter, who lived in Lochgilphead, a village on the shores of Loch Fynn. It was more than a year since he'd last seen them. This surprised me because I knew Matt was married and his wife lived in married quarters in Portsmouth.

However, I decided his extra marital activities were none of my business. I was more interested in what type of car was he going to rent. Plus it would be nice just to get away for a couple of days.

Matt actually borrowed a car from a shipmate on the depot ship. It was a 1957 Wolseley and it appeared to be in good condition. Which was a good thing because Lochgilphead was a hundred miles away over narrow and twisting roads.

We set out on a Friday afternoon in clear sunny weather. My first experience of driving through the Scottish Highlands of Argyll was one of breath taking beauty.

After a short drive to Arrochar we began a long steep climb to the top the of a mountain with a sign at the top that read 'Rest and be Thankful.' Then we began the long precipitous descent to the left bank of Loch Fynn. At the tip of the loch we crossed a hump back bridge and followed a road down the right hand side. The loch is fed from the clear icy streams that cascade down off the surrounding snow-capped highlands.

Motoring along we soon reached Inveraray, which is the residence of the Duke of Argyll and the site of his magnificent and ancient castle. The winding road ran along the waters edge, abreast of rolling fields that were strewn with boulders and thick heather. We passed an occasional lonely crofter's cottage. Sheep dotted the forbidding landscape that swept high onto the towering misty peaks. Driving for approximately four hours, and passing several tiny villages, we finally reach our destination.

My first visit to Lochgilphead was a very pleasant experience and I met many warm and friendly people. Matt had arranged for the both of us to stay with his girlfriend's parents who lived in a four bedroom council house on Brodie Crescent.

I was surprised at how welcome the family made us feel. I was actually expecting a somewhat cooler reception, considering Matt's recent exploits with one of their daughters. Had I not known better I would have thought this was a reunion with their favourite son-in-law. We were treated to a wonderful home cooked meal before heading to a local bar for a few drinks.

Matt's girl friend was named Irene, a girl about my own age. She worked as a nursing aid in a local psychiatric hospital. Her little two-year old daughter Lorraine was very cute and it was easy to understand why Matt wanted to see her. The Campbell family consisted of the parents Angus and Marion, brothers Douglas, Angus and John, sisters Irene and Marie.

Douglas was the eldest and living in Australia but was planning to return home soon. John, at twelve was the youngest and still going to school. Marie was sixteen or seventeen and had not yet begun working. Angus worked for the local electricity dept. He had recently returned from Germany having served two years national service in the army.

The following morning after breakfast Matt, Irene and Lorraine went into the village. Left on my own and feeling like a stranger, I decided to take the car and tour the area. Around lunchtime we all met up at a local pub to down a few pints and play darts. I was pleasantly surprised at the number of the seemingly unattached girls in the bar. That evening we were going to a dance in the village of Ardrishiag, a couple of miles beyond Lochgilphead. I was partnered with a girl name Myra, who lived a few doors down on the crescent.

On the way to the dance we stopped off at another pub. Apparently it was customary to consume several whiskies washed down with pints of ale before dancing.

By the time we arrived at the dance hall I was primed and ready for anything. However, I quickly discovered what I wasn't prepared for, a Highland fling. Fling being the key word. I was also not prepared for the amount of energy that was required.

I was flung around a whirling dance floor amid what sounded like ancient clan's war chants. Nevertheless, I survived, and I actually had a good time.

After the dance I dropped Matt and Irene off at the house, and then I tried it on with Myra in the back seat of the car. Unsuccessfully, I might add.

The next morning I awoke to a throbbing headache and aching muscles, and I was hardly out of bed when Myra arrived. I thought she might have been angry about the previous nights advances, but apparently not. She even suggested that after breakfast we all go for a walk.

Later the four of us dropped into a local pub for lunch, and it was almost 2pm by the time we were ready to drive back to Faslane. Thus ended my first visit to Lochgilphead. It had been great fun and I was invited to come back again soon.

With our sea trials completed we left Scotland to join the 1st Submarine Squadron, based at Fort Blockhouse in Portsmouth. On the 14th May 1960 I was assigned a temporary transfer to HMS Dryad to complete a Navigator Yeoman's course.

But the course had barely started when, on the 27th May, my father died. I received a telegram the following morning and I was immediately released on a week of compassionate leave to attend the funeral.

My father's death was a far greater loss to me than my family ever realised. I'd missed living with him for the first thirteen years of my life, and it was only now that I was beginning to feel a close relationship with him. I was well aware that his illness was terminal, and I should have been prepared for the inevitable. But preparing for the death of someone so close is easier said than done. The loss left me with a feeling of terrible sadness.

He was buried next to our mother at Carnmoney Cemetery. When my mother died in 1939 the family could only afford a simple grave marked by a numbered tag placed on a raised mound of earth. Now that we were slightly better off we raised enough money to have a white marble headstone and surround placed on it.

The day after the funeral, feeling very sorry for myself, I wandered down the

Ballygomartin Road. I wasn't heading in any particular direction, and I had no idea of what to do during the two remaining days of leave.

Lost in a world of my own I almost collided with a girl coming from the opposite direction. As I stopped to apologise I thought she looked familiar, then I realised she was the young girl who, a few years earlier, had called me 'Rock'.

I blushed as I clumsily apologized and explain who I was. With a warm and friendly smile she said she was fine. She offered her sympathy saying how sorry she was for the loss of my father. We stood there for what seemed like an eternity as I struggled to make small talk.

I knew I wasn't being very suave with this pretty young girl. Her name was Eleanor and she was on her way home from work. I was so taken by her that I ask to walk her home. On the way to her house I learned that she was training as a seamstress at Ewarts Mill. She was only fifteen, but her sixteenth birthday was only a month away on the 26th June. I made a mental note of the date, planning to send a card when I got back to Portsmouth.

As I walked along with Eleanor my head must have been in the clouds because I stumbled when she stopped at her front gate. We stood in another awkward silence while I searched for the courage to ask her out.

That evening, after supper, I arrived for my first date with Eleanor, and when she opened the door to greet me she took my breath away. When I'd met her earlier coming from work I thought she was beautiful. Now she was absolutely gorgeous.

That evening was the first of our many visits to the Stadium cinema on the corner of Tennant Street. Later, after the show, standing at her front door we embraced and I kissed her gently. I think this was her first real kiss.

I was very disappointed when she told me she was going to a Gospel meeting the following evening with a couple of friends. She didn't want to let them down, but then added that I was welcome to come along too. I politely declined; Gospel meetings were not my style. There was a wave of these Gospel meetings going on in Belfast at the time, promoting what they termed as 'Good Living'. Their list of sins included going to the cinema, pubs and dancing. They regularly handed out religious tracts and preached to lines of people outside cinemas on Friday and Saturday nights.

I was keen to spend time with Eleanor, but not at a Gospel meeting. I was already guilty of their first three sins

On Sunday evening I had to catch the steamer back to England. Eleanor and I met in the afternoon and we went for a walk. We rode the bus to the city limits at Legoniel. Then, hand in hand, we followed a pathway onto the surrounding hills to look down on our grand old city. When we returned home around suppertime our last kiss was more of a peck than an ardent embrace. I realised that, because it was still daylight, Eleanor was too shy to be seen kissing in public. We said our sad farewell, promising to write each other as often as possible.

On my return to Dryad I joined another class that allowed me to complete the yeoman course. I eventually rejoined the Taciturn on 18th June 1960, just in time to sail for Londonderry.

I was pleased about visiting Derry as there would be the opportunity of a weekend leave, and I could see Eleanor again. I remembered to send her a birthday card, and I'd also posted a couple of letters.

We were on exercise somewhere North of Scotland, and as usual the weather was foul. We were scheduled to spend two weekends in Derry, but the first was delayed by bad weather and we docked on a Saturday afternoon, too late to get home for the weekend.

On the second visit we arrived on time, and I was granted weekend leave. It was between paydays so I had to hitchhike the eighty miles to Belfast. I arrived home at roughly 8 pm and immediately called on Eleanor. We enjoyed an all too brief but happy two days together. On Sunday, to be safe, I left at noon to hitch back to the boat. It was my lucky day. No sooner had I put my thumb up when an RN ambulance heading to Derry stopped and gave me a lift, right to the dockyard gates. Once again it was back to the North Sea and more hard work. In my off duty moments I would lie on my bunk and let my thoughts wander back to Eleanor. For the first time since Margaret I was beginning to believe I could fall in love again. I knew I had to be cautious and take things slowly. Eleanor was only sixteen and hardly old enough for serious involvement. Margaret was still a painful memory, and I didn't want to set myself up for the same hurt again.

I thought the Navy must be co-operating with my new romance when I learned of our next destination. The Taciturn was scheduled to dock in Belfast for a few days in July. I was over the moon to actually be sailing into my hometown. I arranged for my sister Anna and Eleanor to visit the boat while we were alongside. I first carefully explained why they should not wear skirts for the visit.

When a submarine was opened to visitors, it was a race to stand at the bottom of the torpedo-loading hatch to help the ladies down the ladder. In harbour, when the batteries are being charged, air is drawn though the conning tower hatch. It causes an updraft at the forward hatch, where the visitors enter. The popular style of the wide skirt of the sixties often made them difficult to control in high winds. Can you can imagine the effect on a skirt from the air blowing up through the hatch while a girl climbs down. The unfortunate girl needed both hands to grip the handrails, which left her with no means of controlling her billowing skirt. It was marvellous fun and a great view for the sailors below. Little concern was given to our unfortunate and embarrassed young victims. In the case of Anna and Eleanor I made very sure they would not be embarrassed. They would wear trousers. The tour of the boat didn't impress the girls very much. Anna remarked that it must be like living in a sewer pipe.

After Belfast it was back to Portsmouth for some minor repairs before joining an NATO exercise in the Atlantic. Although the Taciturn was built during the war, her age didn't detract from the fact that she was still quite a remarkable vessel. In the early fifties she had undergone an extensive refit and conversion. The old conning tower and 4inch deck gun were removed and replaced with a streamline fin. The pressure hull was cut in two and an extension inserted to lengthen the boat. The extra length provided space for another bank of batteries. This resulted in a very fast boat, capable of some eighteen knots underwater, a speed that was unheard of in a diesel electric submarine at the time. No wonder they were known as 'Super T's. However, it was a speed only to be used in an emergency because at eighteen knots the batteries drained in about thirty minutes.

I only experienced this amazing burst of speed once during my time on board. Lurking around the Bay of Biscay in the late autumn of 1960, we were positioned to attack an aircraft carrier task force. During the early morning watch I picked up a large radar contact that was determined to be the enemy force. As the contact closed it separated into a circle of several smaller contacts with three larger ones inside. I counted approximately twenty ships. A huge screen of escorts positioned around a carrier and two cruisers. The Skipper, using the smaller attack periscope, did a quick sweep to judge the situation. He decided to stay at periscope depth and attempt to sneak inside the circle between two frigates. The plan went well for the first few minutes and we glided silently past the escorts. Suddenly all hell broke loose as we were hit by several sonar pings from three or four ships. The game was up and if we waited around we would certainly be declared sunk.

That was when I experienced the power of our extra battery. Going to full ahead we turned and dived to two hundred feet in what seemed like seconds. Inside the boat it was almost like flying as we banked hard over and surged forward. In no time at all we were clear of the searching escorts and well outside the screen.

We slowed to three knots and crept away, thinking perhaps we'd get another chance later. As it happened we never contacted the enemy force again. We had not failed completely, though. At the exercise debriefing it was noted that the only boat to penetrate the screen and live was the Taciturn.

The exercises continued throughout the remainder of the year because of the growing concern over the increasing Cold War brinkmanship.

Over Christmas of 1960 I was home on two weeks leave, and all of it was spent with Eleanor. On Christmas Eve as I was seeing Eleanor home she handed me a gift wrapped neatly in Christmas paper. She told me not to open it until the following morning. When I opened it the next morning I found a lovely Ronson cigarette lighter. But what really made the gift so special were the words engraved on it. 'My Love Always, Eleanor'. Even though I'd recently quite smoking this was something I'd always cherish and carry with me. Through the holidays we danced and saw several films, but our favourite time was just sitting in the parlour playing records. The front parlour in our house was seldom used and was mostly available whenever we wanted it. I'd light the fire in the later afternoon and by the time Eleanor arrived the room would be cosy and warm.

In the dim lighting we'd listen to Perry Como, Jimmy Rodgers and Doris Day singing their latest hits. We'd sit together on the sofa with our arms around each other talking, petting and kissing. These were warm and tender moments, which are rarely experienced beyond the prime of one's youth.

When my leave was over Eleanor came to the docks to see me off. We kissed one last time before I headed for the gangway. It was a warm and loving embrace. Eleanor was no longer quite so shy as when we'd first kissed in daylight. She handed me the photo I'd been pestering her for. I wanted to have it above my bunk where I'd see it each time I turned in. I was in love again, and a bounce had returned to my step.

With Eleanor's photo fixed above my bunk I was soon back in the North Sea on NATO exercises.

The North Sea is usually rough and cold, and it makes submarine operations very difficult. At periscope depth, in gale force conditions, we sometimes broke the surface, and this would cause our Skipper to go ballistic. In wartime, breaking the surface unintentionally could result in you being detected, which might result in the loss of the boat.

Living on a submarine in such dreadful weather conditions was also very unpleasant. The chef was often unable to provide us with a hot meal.

During these exercises the submarine's actions were always covert. We were the enemy, and just using the periscope could put us at risk of being detected. So surfacing to recharge the batteries was out of the question. This left us with only one option, and that was snorting. Snorting enabled us to draw fresh air into the boat and run the diesel engines, which in turn recharged the batteries. Although the snort mast operates much like a periscope, it has a much larger profile making it even more prone to detection. For that reason we only snorted after dark.

The problem with snorting in heavy seas is that it can cause some very unpleasant things to happen. For instance, if the snort dips below a wave, a valve snaps shut and cuts off the air, and this causes the diesels to shut down.

And in the few moments that it takes for the diesels to actually stop, they draw air from inside the boat creating a vacuum. Sleeping shipmates were often awoken abruptly with extreme pain in their eardrums. There would be a chorus of extremely colourful curses from the accommodation compartment, heaping blame on those who were supposed to be controlling the depth.

After a couple of weeks on such an exercise the conditions on the boat deteriorates and the crew become filthy, tired and often antagonistic. Arguments over the most silly and petty issues often erupted on the mess decks, and it took the intervention of cooler heads to stop them getting out of control.

Sometimes the flagship would call a brief halt to the exercise and order the submarines to the surface. While this was probably done with the best of intentions, it actually had the opposite effect on us. The Admiral probably thought we'd all come rushing out on to the deck for some much needed fresh air. But the problem was that a submarine on the surface in rough seas had as much water washing over it as it had under it. Going out onto the upper deck would have been suicidal.

Serving meals and most other tasks were all but impossible inside the pitching boat. A submarine is designed for stealth and silent running beneath the waves. On the surface, in heavy seas, it reacts like flat-bottomed barge.

But all exercises do eventually come to an end, and we were ordered to Faslane for repairs, and some welcome shore leave for the crew. Once again I was on my way home for Easter. I spent all of my two weeks leave with Eleanor. We did all the usual things, went to the pictures, went to the dances, and sat in the front parlour playing records. I borrowed an old car from a friend and we drove down to Dublin for the day, just before I had to return to duty.

During the summer of 1961 we mostly operated in the North Atlantic. There was a lot of concern about the cold war, and the fact that it appeared to be escalating.

Moscow and Washington were engaged in a dangerous game of brinkmanship, and our sea time and patrols increased accordingly. We spent most of our time sailing around the areas between Ireland and Iceland, listening for and attempting to track any Russian boats that might be heading out into the Atlantic.

To refuel and take on supplies we occasionally docked at Faslane, which was always a welcome respite. Matt and I planned another visit to Lochgilphead and we invited two of our shipmates, Michael Foster and Michael Chislett, to come with us.

Michael Chislett had only recently joined the Taciturn. He and I had quickly become good friends.

Getting to and from Lochgilphead wasn't always easy. The weather was often bad and we couldn't always afford to rent a car. Hitching a ride in the Highlands was never the simple answer either. The traffic was scarce and not everyone stopped. Wearing a uniform did improve our chances but nevertheless we still ended up doing a lot of walking. The biggest worry was getting back to the to base on time. With no guarantee of a ride, we ran the risk of missing the boat.

During one of these long and lonely walks the idea of buying another car began to grow. However the problem with owning a car whilst you were serving in the Navy was where you were going to keep it.

Portsmouth was our homeport and the obvious place. But a car in Portsmouth wasn't much use if I was in Scotland. I'd been saving for some time and the money was starting to burn a hole in my pocket. It was time to go in search of a car.

I'd owned several ancient and unreliable pre-war cars of 1930's vintage, but this time I was determined to find a Morris Minor, Austin A35, or a Hillman Minx from the 1950's era. Unfortunately my savings didn't match my desire. Those small cars, which were easy on petrol, were also in demand and they fetched a good price. On one sales lot I saw a clear example of this. A cheap and cheerful Morris Minor was selling for £1000, parked next to it was a luxury Mk 9 Jaguar with a price of £500. Both were 1956 models and in similar condition with low mileage. I couldn't afford either one and certainly couldn't have afforded the petrol to run a big Jag. I finally settled for a very nice 1952 Morris Isis four door saloon with a six-cylinder engine for around a hundred pounds. It was finished in beautiful black gloss paint, with lots of chrome, but what really impressed me was the fact that it had a radio. I'd never owned a car with a radio before.

I was very proud of my new acquisition and I spent as much time polishing it as I did driving it. But I only had a few days to enjoy it before we sailed into the North Atlantic once again. I tucked it in behind the accommodation block, locked it up and prayed that it would remain safe and sound until I returned.

Chapter 11
Ouch! That Really Hurt

Throughout the remainder of the summer we exercised in the North Atlantic, working closely with many NATO units.

To break the monotony of constantly being hunted by a fleet of anti-submarine vessels, we made brief weekend trips to Gibraltar, and near the end of August we visited the French port of Lorient.

The town had been a major U-Boat base during the Second World War. The huge submarine pens were impressive concrete structures, with heavy steel doors that were designed to withstand the most determined raid. Once inside the pens the German boats were able to refit, rearm and refuel in complete safety. I was disappointed that we were berthed at a wharf and not in one of the pens. I can't say Lorient was one of my more memorable shore runs. Sidewalk cafes serving wine was popular with the locals, but there were no English style pubs, no best bitter and no darts. The language was a problem too and the locals were not particularly friendly. It was probably due to Allied actions during the war. Churchill had ordered the destruction of the French fleet before Hitler could use it. Lorient and other ports being used by the U-Boats were subjected to constant heavy bombing. The raids cost the lives of many French sailors and civilians. It was an unfortunate necessity of war. I tried understanding why we received such a cool reception, but it wasn't easy. I felt like asking them where they thought they'd be today if we hadn't done those things.

The following weekend we visited the port of Brest. It was much like Lorient, and the people had a similar cool attitude towards us. I suppose I should have expected it, history has shown the French and English were never the best of friends.

On a Sunday evening I was on duty watch, and preparing the boat for an early departure the following morning. I was in the forward torpedo compartment installing two of the three 'strong backs' below the torpedo-loading hatch. On British submarines and in fact most submarines in general, the torpedo-loading hatch is the weakest point of the pressure hull. The problem is the length of the torpedoes, they are at least 20ft, and have to be loaded at an angle.

The loading hatch is fitted over the pressure hull at approximately a thirty-degree angle to enable the torpedo to pass into the compartment. This creates an oblong hole in the pressure hull, that is much weaker than the usual round type of hatch The 'strong backs' are inserted across the oblong gap to take up the pressure when the boat dives. I was only installing two for the moment leaving enough space for the sailors coming from shore to enter through the hatch. The third would be installed in the morning when the hatch was shut.

A 'strong back' is a solid iron bar that weighs roughly one hundred pounds. It is necessary to use the ladder to reach the insert points. I lifted the first one above my head and it slipped neatly into place without a problem.

For the second one I had to step higher up the ladder and as I was about to slip it into place I nearly lost my footing. I arched my back as I desperately attempted to control my balance and felt a sharp pain at the base of my spine. Somehow I managed to hold on and slip the bar into place.

The panic was over. Had I dropped the 'strong back' it would have gone right through the deck plates and probably caused major damage. Or worse it might have struck a shipmate.

The next morning when they called the hands at 0500hrs I rolled over to swing my legs out of the bunk and almost fainted from the sudden pain. I remained perfectly still and flat on my back afraid to move again. Of course, no one believed that I was in pain. The duty Petty Officer eventually stopped shouting at me and informed the coxswain I was ill. I wasn't ill! I was simply unable to move without causing myself severe pain.

Once we cleared the harbour and the boat dived, the coxswain arrived to find out what was wrong with me. I'd managed to struggle out of my bunk but I could only sit upright keeping very still. The slightest movement caused me awful pain.

Submarines didn't carry medical personnel and the coxswain was responsible for giving first aid and administering medication. Medication at sea usually meant a couple of codeine tablets. That's just what I received, plus a bandage wrapped around my waist.

The bandage offered no support to my back and merely rolled into a ball around my middle when

I moved. It was decided that I should be transferred to the depot ship to see a Medical Officer.

Transferring someone from a submarine at sea is an ordeal even when the person is fully fit. For me climbing to the bridge and inching myself into a small boat that rolled heavily with the sea motion was total agony. The whaler took me to the depot ship and I finally made it to the sick bay. After a cursory exam the doctor said I had a slipped disc. I was to stay on board the depot ship resting in the sick bay for a week. The treatment I received during this time was to sleep on a hard board instead of a mattress. At the end of the week I was declared 'fit for light duties' and returned to the Taciturn. I didn't bother explaining to the doctor there was no such thing as light duties on a submarine. I was dragging my right leg noticeably when I left the ship to rejoin the Taciturn.

Slowly the pain subsided and my back recovered, and soon I was walking normally again. I was young and healthy, and I quickly forgot about the whole episode.

I never imagined it would return some ten years later and affect me for the rest of my life.

My growing friendship with Michael Chislett was proving to be an added bonus. He was a competent submariner, and being a few years my senior he acted as my mentor. Through his friendship and patience I learned so much about the submarine trade.

Before joining the Taciturn, Michael had served with the 6th Submarine Squadron in Canada. In 1958 he'd met and married a lovely young Nova Scotia girl named Betty, and he was very excited when his wife finally arrived in England. They rented a small flat in

Gosport. They already had a son named Paul and a second baby was on the way.

On the 4th September Betty gave birth to a baby girl who they named Tina. But things don't always go as expected when one is in the navy. A few days after Tina's birth the Taciturn was transferred to Devonport. Michael and Betty had hardly settled into their Gosport flat when they had to move all over again. It turned out okay because Michael was almost immediately allocated a house in the new base married-quarters.

The first time I met Betty was in the autumn of 1961. One Saturday Michael was on duty and worried about Betty because she had only moved into the new home a few days earlier. He asked me to pop in and see if she needed anything and make sure that she was okay. Betty was a shy and very young twenty year old who was still learning to deal with to the strange ways of the English.

When I first saw her, she was standing on her front door step struggling with a handful of coins as she tried to pay the milkman. She appeared to be having difficulty understanding his odd West Country accent. I had arrived in the nick of time to save the situation. Extracting three shillings and sixpence from her fistful of change I paid the amused milkman.

That morning was the beginning of a friendship that continues to this day. I was often invited to their home to enjoy Betty's fine cooking, and I was quickly elevated to honorary uncle to the children.

When we were away from our homeport, which was often, Michael and I spent most of our shore time together. As friends go we were quite inseparable and we enjoyed many a good time. I trusted Michael and

I often relied upon his advice. Unfortunately I didn't always follow it.

At the same time Matt Smalley's wife had put her foot down declaring that Lochgilphead was out of bounds for him. On the next visit to Faslane with Matt grounded I asked Michael to come with me instead. I thought he'd enjoyed our last visit and was surprised when he said no. He told me that I'd be wise to give Lochgilphead, and in particular Irene, a wide berth. I just laughed insisting that I wasn't interested or involved with Irene, and that visiting the village was just a bit of fun.

My old Ganges shipmate Michael Foster was smitten with Marie, Irene's younger sister, and he was spending a lot of time in Lochgilphead. A few weeks before Christmas leave was due to start he announced he was getting married.

The wedding was planned for Boxing Day, 26th December 1961, and I was invited. I would have rather gone home but couldn't let my shipmate down on his special day. I wrote to Eleanor saying I couldn't get home for Christmas. I didn't go into details and left her to assume I was on duty. It was a guilty letter because in truth I was lying without actually saying anything. My invitation to the wedding came with a few strings attached. I was asked to rent a car and drive some of the wedding party to Scotland. Matt Smalley was to be his best man and he was coming with his wife. I wondered what might happen when his two women met.

It was arranged that I pick up the Smalley's first, then drive to Epsom and collect Michael's mother and his sister. Naturally everyone was expected to share the cost of the car rental and the fuel.

But problems started when I tried to rent the car. The Christmas rush was in full swing and there was nothing suitable available. All I could get was a battered old Bedford van with only two seats in the front. I wasn't too concerned because one of the seats was the driver's. I decided Michael's mother could have the other one, and everyone else could sit on cushions, or on their luggage, in the back.

A few days before Christmas, with my passengers safely on board, the old van lumbered along the Great Northern Highway heading for the Border and the Scottish

Lowlands. I drove straight through, only stopping for food and petrol, and we arrived in Lochgilphead late that evening.

Totally exhausted, I turned in almost immediately. The next morning Irene awoke me with a cup of tea and a fresh bread roll. She sat on the edge of my bed and talked about the upcoming wedding. I was tempted to ask her how she felt about meeting Matt's wife but I decided it was none of my business.

However, the two women kept their distance throughout the celebrations, surprisingly no sparks flew and no hair was pulled.

On the morning of the wedding my head throbbed from too much whiskey and beer at Michaels stag party the night before. After shaving, bathing and donning in my uniform I felt a little better. When I entered the living room I was met with a situation of chaos. It was impossible to hear what was being said above the din. Did you phone the photographer? Have the flowers arrived? I need a safety pin. Who ironed this?

It was a mad house. Clothes were hanging everywhere, on the furniture, on the doors, on the mantelpiece. The room was strewn with women's gowns, hats, coats and shoes. Apart from me there wasn't another male to be seen.

It only took me a fraction of a second to assess the situation, and clear out. The pubs were open and it wasn't long before I met up with Angus, Douglas and Matt. Douglas had only recently returned from Australia, and he was struggling to establish who was married to whom. He thought Irene was married to Matt because of Lorraine. I did my best to avoid his questions and not become involved in the conversation. The men were already dressed and ready for the 2 pm wedding ceremony. Until then it seemed wise to remain in the relative safety of the pub, where we sank a few pints while waiting to go to the church. Irene arrived on the scene about thirty minutes before the ceremony was due to begin, and she brought carnations with her to pin on our lapels.

On our way to the reception I was surprised when Irene caught up with me and took my arm. I just put it down to being friendly. Everything had gone off without a hitch. The flowers had come on time, the photographer had arrived, and most important the bride turned up. I wondered if the earlier search for a safety pin had contributed to the day's success.

More photographs were taken at the reception with the bride and groom cutting the cake. Next came a variety of speeches and toasts, and finally, later that evening, the bride and groom left for their honeymoon.

The place was awash with whiskey and beer, and I had my share. I was celebrating enthusiastically, and later in the evening I somehow ended up wearing a kilt. I'm not sure how that happened but it's possible that I traded my uniform with Angus.

I was certainly no fashion statement wearing a kilt, and I definitely didn't capture the Rob Roy look. I seemed to recall that Irene had been involved in the exchange of the costumes. I'd flatly refused to go completely native and she called me a chicken, insisting that real Scotsman didn't wear anything under their kilt. I might have been thoroughly inebriated and barely functioning but I retained enough dignity to hang on to my underpants.

It was in the early morning hours when I eventually arrived home and found my bed. In literally one movement I undressed and collapsed onto the bed. Moments later I was aware of Irene slipping in beside me. The next morning I awoke alone suffering from another vicious, self-inflicted hangover.

The memories of the previous night were at best a little vague, and I struggled to fill in the blanks. How did Irene end up in my bed? Did I ask her? Was it her idea or mine? I just didn't know, and maybe she didn't remember either. Neither one of us was sober. But regardless of how it happened, it was time to get up and face the world.

I had to pack the van, round up my passengers and leave at no later than 10 am. I had promised to pick up the newly weds at their hotel and drop them off in Glasgow.

The silent and empty living room was a huge contrast from yesterday. Margaret and her mother's luggage were already in the front hall, and they were in the kitchen finishing a last cup of tea. I couldn't face food right then, but a cup of strong hot tea went down very well.

Once I'd loaded the luggage we had to go and collect Matt and his wife. They were lodging with friends at the other end of the village. There was no sign of life in the Campbell household. The brothers were probably laying low nursing their hangovers. I'd have been doing the same if I didn't have to leave so early.

As I started the van Irene and her mother appeared at the front door to bid us farewell. They were still dressed in nightgowns and robes with their hair and makeup looking somewhat the worse for wear. I guessed they were probably suffering the same morning-after symptoms as me.

I opened the window and waved as I shouted goodbye. Irene smiled and said something that I couldn't hear. It was too late now, I had the van moving and heading out onto the main road.

We picked up Michael and Marie in the village of Minard, about five miles away. The return trip was long, quiet and uneventful, and I was glad when I reached to the end of the trip and returned the van.

Safely back in Portsmouth the recent excitement in Lochgilphead quickly faded from memory. A pile of mail was waiting for me back on the Taciturn, including a Christmas card and a letter from Eleanor.

In early January of 1962 we sailed back into the miserable weather of the North Atlantic.

While sitting in the forward torpedo compartment one evening drinking tea I told Michael Chislett about my recent adventures. He warned me again that I was asking for trouble. What happens if you get her pregnant? I shrugged this off saying I was being careful, and knew what I was doing. Besides, it was only a bit of fun and certainly nothing serious.

When we later docked in Gibraltar for a few days rest the first thing I looked for was mail from home. I received two letters from Eleanor and I opened them immediately, and in my enthusiasm didn't notice the one from Irene. Eleanor was fine. She had missed me over Christmas and went on to tell all about the holidays and the gifts she received etc. That was when I noticed the letter from Irene and I suddenly felt very guilty about my deception.

Irene's letter was very flattering, saying how much she had enjoyed being with me. She said she was missing me, and she could hardly wait until my next visit. She invited me to spend Easter leave with her. I could travel up with Michael. I was aware that with a shipmate married to her sister it would be difficult making excuses. She'd be aware of my every move. Michael would write to Marie, and she would pass all the news on to Irene.

I had no intentions of spending Easter in Scotland, but at the same time I was reluctant to hurt her feelings. I still wasn't sure how events had unfolded at Christmas. I was even less sure of how Irene actually viewed our relationship. I decided to write and tell her that I was going home for Easter, as it had been six months since I'd last been home. It was the honest answer and solved the issue for the moment. At the end of March we returned to Plymouth for maintenance and to allow the crew leave. I travelled home for my two weeks leave and at once realised how much I had missed Eleanor. The reunion was a heady time for both of us and we were surely in love. We spent every free minute together and I must confess the temptation to propose was very strong. But I had to control the urge, after all Eleanor was still only seventeen. When I returned aboard the Taciturn later she was all I could think about.

Then incredibly in August Michael Foster talked me into going to Scotland for summer leave. I can't explain this stupidity, I had the most wonderful girl waiting for me in Belfast and here I was driving to Scotland. I was certainly not in love with Irene, but sex was a powerful motivation.

Back in Plymouth in September and on weekend leave I was offered a ride to Portsmouth by a Canadian submariner who had just purchased a new Vauxhall Victor with left hand drive steering. He was eager to take the new car out onto the highway and give it a good run. He was due to return to Canada soon and he had ordered the car especially so he could take it home with him.

He and his wife were visiting friends and they had plenty of room for me. We set out on a Saturday morning with the three of us sitting on the front bench seat.

Driving in the UK while sitting on the right hand side of a left hand drive car is a little bit disconcerting. As the passenger you are the first to be exposed to the oncoming traffic when trying to over take.

About ten miles out of Plymouth we joined a stretch of dual carriageway and gradually increased speed. Humming along at about 60 mph we were relaxed and enjoying the ride. Approaching a slow moving lorry in the inside lane we pulled out to overtake. Suddenly and without warning the lorry pulled out directly across our path. What a strange feeling it is when you realise you're about to crash.

My life passed before my eyes as we raced toward the lorry. The next thing I was aware of is lying on the grass with people standing all around me. I couldn't see much because my head was bleeding and the blood was running into my eyes. I was vaguely aware of being lifted onto a stretcher and placed in an ambulance. Then blackness.

Somewhere far off I could hear singing, but I couldn't seem to focus. Through a strange fog I was aware of five or six angels standing and singing nearby. Was I dead and in Heaven? A sudden surge of pain made me realise that I was still alive. But I still couldn't explain the angels or why they were singing. As my head cleared I realised that it was Sunday morning. I was in a hospital ward with a Church service in progress. The angels were choirboys dressed in white gowns.

I had been unconscious for about sixteen hours after being transported back to Plymouth to the RN Hospital. I had twelve stitches in my heavily bandaged forehead. I was also very aware of pain that seemed to radiate from a variety of cuts and bruises.

The following Tuesday morning two doctors came to remove the bandage from my forehead, and they seem a bit concerned about the nasty gash. The twelve original stitches had only been temporary to close the deep wound. They felt that a more permanent repair was needed. They explained that this was an opportune time because a Plastic Surgeon on Naval Reserve duty was available.

So on Wednesday morning it was back to the operating theatre. When I awoke later I had thirty-two stitches in a much tidier wound. Looking in a mirror it appeared as though I had a zipper on my forehead.

About ten days later the stitches were taken out, and it was extremely painful. I was wishing I only had the original twelve stitches instead of thirty-two. Nevertheless, my scar looked so much better. It was still red and angry but the doctor assured me it would soon fade.

I remained in hospital for three weeks, and I was then sent home on three weeks sick leave. Michael Chislett had come to visit earlier and he informed me I was off the Taciturn and returning to HMS Dolphin as unfit for sea duty after my leave.

Whilst I was home on leave my brother-in-law Dan suggested I visit a lawyer and claim damages for my injuries. I didn't have the slightest idea of the legal aspects of an accident, so Dan took me to see his solicitor. I gave him all the information I had, but my only real evidence was a small cutting that I'd taken from a newspaper. The lawyer took a note of this and said he'd be in touch if he had any news.

I spent the next three weeks enjoying my unexpected leave in the company of Eleanor.

When I returned to Dolphin I was given a brief exam by the base MO who declared me fit for sea. Within a few days I was travelling north to join the submarine Otter. She was just completing a refit in Greenock. The fact that I couldn't wear my uniform cap had not been taken into consideration. I simply could not tolerate wearing any type of headdress. Every time the rim touched my scar I suffered extreme shooting pains across the top of my head. When I explained this to the coxswain I was sent to see the Medical Officer on the submarine depot ship.

He was a young and modern thinking doctor, and he believed he could cure me by using hypnosis. It didn't work, so finally he recommended I be returned to the Haslar Naval Hospital. I was on my way back to Dolphin having spent barely three weeks on the Otter.

A medical specialist at Haslar explained that my problem was caused by nerve damage. When nerves are severed in an accident such as I had experienced they often become frayed. He was most sympathetic when he explained the remedy and cure for my problem. For the next three weeks I attended his surgery every morning for half an hour of treatment. The treatment consisted of lying on a bed while the scar was hammered to deaden the nerve ends. The hammer was the type used for testing a person's knee reflex, but it felt like a sledgehammer to me. I had to remain on the bed for about an hour after the treatment just to recover.

December arrived and I was home again on Christmas leave. It was wonderful to be free of the hammer for two weeks, and being with Eleanor was tonic enough to deaden my woes for the duration of my leave.

The new year of 1963 saw me back in Dolphin, still unable to wear a cap for any length of time. Walking around a Naval base whilst not wearing a cap is an absolute nightmare. It's guaranteed to cause every passing Officer, Chief Petty Officer and Petty Officer to stop you with the howl of, " Where's your headdress lad? Put your cap on, boy. Who do you think you are walking around the base out of uniform?"

Of course I had a chit stating that I was excused wearing a cap, and it was almost worn out from having been produced so many times.

Finally in March I was able to wear a cap, and I was promptly declared fit for sea duty and posted to 'spare crew' at Dolphin. The base held a spare crew in case a boat needed a replacement for a sick or injured member in her crew. The spare crew guaranteed that a replacement was readily available.

It was late in the day by the time I picked up all my transfer documents from the Regulating Office. I needed to file papers with the pay office and the fleet mail office if I expected to be paid or receive mail. But the first and most important task was to move into the 'spare crew' quarters. I had to draw bedding, find an empty bunk and transfer my kit, and by the time I'd done this it was very late. I decided to leave the rest of my routine until the following morning. That night I turned in early and quickly fell asleep.

Suddenly a blinding light was shinning in my eyes. Behind the light someone's voice is yelling, "Are you Rodgers? You've got ten minutes to get your ass on board the Totem. She's about to sail."

I arrived just as they were removing the gangway. I was unshaven, unwashed and now underway. The boat was heading out to operate in the Irish Sea, with a visit to the City of Cork on the weekend. Thursday at sea was payday, and everyone was paid. Except me! My pay documents were sitting in my locker back at Dolphin. I was broke, with perhaps five shillings to my name. The chance of borrowing some funds from a shipmate was nil. I was not a permanent member of the crew, so lending me money would be too high a risk. I could disappear just as quickly as I had arrived.

Alongside in Cork on the Saturday morning, I was off duty and free to go ashore.

Directly opposite the gangway was a pub and although it didn't official open until noon, a discrete tap on a side door and we were ushered inside.

The blinds were still down so the interior was pretty dim as we ordered pints of Guinness and headed for a table by the fireside. As our eyes adjusted to the gloom we jumped when we saw a Garda (Irish policeman) standing at the bar.

"Is it British sailors breaking the law I'm seeing here?"

We froze on the spot. After a dramatic pause he continued, "Ah well, sure wouldn't it be breaking the law to let salty young seafarers like yourselves to go thirsty."

A couple of pints later and my funds considerably reduced I decide to return on board for lunch. The levity in the seamen's mess usually increases after the daily issue of a tot of rum. This certainly was the case aboard the Totem. So of course someone had to suggest we head out of town to Blarney Castle to kiss the famous stone. Having imbibed a tot of rum and two pints of Guinness, kissing the Blarney Stone seemed like an admirable idea.

The bus fare depleted my dwindling funds by a further sixpence. Arriving at the castle we were directed to climb a circular stairway to the top of the tower where we found the Blarney Stone, and an enterprising photographer. Who, for one shilling would take a photo of our lips touching this famous stone. We readily agreed. We had to have a record of the event. But after paying the photographer I couldn't afford the return bus fare and I had to walk the five or so miles back to the city. I returned on board depressed, and with my pockets empty and feet aching.

The city was hosting a dance for the crew that evening, and it promised lots of girls in attendance. But even if my sore feet had recovered in time I still wouldn't be doing any dancing. I was broke.

When I entered the mess I noticed the mail had arrived. I showed no interest, my change of address was with my pay doc's back at Dolphin. Therefore I was stunned when a shipmate asked if I'd got my letter. What letter? It had to be a mistake. It couldn't be for me.

Nevertheless, on the table lay a large official looking white envelope with my name neatly typed, and HMS Dolphin as my address. I quickly tore it open to find it contained several typed pages. What immediately caught my attention, though, was the attached cheque.

The letter was from my lawyer back in Belfast. I had long since forgotten all about my visit to his office. Yet here it was, a settlement for my injuries in the sum of one thousand pounds. Never in my life had I held such a huge sum of money in my hands. The first question that came to mind was how it had reached me. The fleet mail office didn't have my present address. Then it occurred to me that only a few hours earlier I'd spent my last few coins kissing the Blarney Stone. Now I was rich beyond my wildest dreams. Was this a coincidence? Or was it the luck of the Irish?

I'm sure you will have already guessed that I did make it to the dance that night.

Two weeks later I was back in the 'spare crew' mess at Dolphin, waiting to begin my Easter leave. My recent wealth had me going in different directions trying to decide how to spend it. Eleanor was foremost on my mind. Was the time right to buy her a ring and propose? I was a little hesitant because she was still only eighteen. But she would be nineteen in June, was that old enough? Would her parents approve? Would my family approve? For days I struggled with these questions, finally deciding to wait until my leave in August. By then she'd be nineteen, and I thought that was a more acceptable age for a girl to marry.

For Easter I bought Eleanor a silver bracelet inset with small diamonds. They probably weren't genuine, but they looked real enough and came in a blue velvet presentation case that looked very expensive. I gave it to Eleanor on our first night together. She was delighted and hugged me tightly, and in that brief moment I wished I had bought the engagement ring instead. It took all of my will power not to blurt out that I wanted to marry her. But it was a big decision and the timing had to be just right. Years later looking back on this moment I'm reminded of an old saying 'He who hesitates.'

But at Easter in 1963, I was happy and my thoughts were carefree and the future looked rosy.

Chapter 12
The Trap is Set

After Easter leave I rejoined the 'spare crew' at Dolphin, and I remained there until June without any more early morning awakenings, or sudden departures to sea.

In June I began a new radar course at the RP2 level, which ran for roughly ten weeks. Everything went well, and just as I was preparing to sit the final exam in late August I received a surprise draft notice. The submarine HMS Alcide was about to complete a major refit in Rosyth and they urgently required a radar operator. I was ordered to join her immediately on completion of the course.

My summer leave was cancelled and I was quite upset wondering how to go about making the necessary adjustments to my plans. In the New Year after Alcide successfully completed her sea trials she was due to sail to Canada. In the meantime I had to find a way to propose to Eleanor and explain the urgency of the situation. If we could arrange the marriage over Christmas leave then the Navy would allow Eleanor to follow me to Canada later. I left Dolphin on the 22nd August catching the night train to Edinburgh, and during the long journey I thought of a workable plan to propose and hopefully marry Eleanor within the time limitations. My solution was really quite simple. All I had to do was propose by telephone and explain the need for haste. But things are never as simple as they first appear. I didn't know the phone number of Dan's shop, and it was the only telephone available. I'd have to write home and ask for the number and explain why I needed it. Writing home and receiving a reply would take at least two weeks. Next I'd have to set up a time and day when Eleanor could be at the shop to take the call. I was sure Noel could arrange to have her there on a Saturday or Sunday morning at an agreed time. But that too would take the best part of another two weeks to arrange. Then another snag occurred to me, what if we were delayed at sea on the morning I was supposed to ring. While we were completing our trials in Scotland there was always a risk of delays or changes. The safe answer was to wait until we returned to Portsmouth in early November. The time remaining would be short but it could still work. I'd agree to any and all arrangement Eleanor made, I'd marry her in a church a registry office or anywhere else. The worst possible outcome would be a long engagement and a wedding when I returned from Canada. It wasn't my first choice but not completely unacceptable either.

I arrived at Rosyth Dockyard the following morning feeling quite happy with my plans. Returning to Rosyth was in a strange sort of a way like a homecoming. As a little boy during the war I had lived in Rosyth for about a year, and though my memory of the place was vague many places felt familiar. One thing I did recall vividly was the Forth Bridge. I had been so impressed as a child when we first crossed it by train. I remembered sticking my head out of the carriage window to get a better view and crying because I got soot in my eye.

I wasn't surprised to find that the Alcide was a hive of activity when I arrived. That was the usual state for a submarine when she was nearing the end of a refit. The Head's of departments would be getting anxious as they waited for essential parts to arrive, wondering if they could be installed on time.

No time was wasted in putting me to work. As a senior leading hand I was appointed Second Coxswain. I was quite pleased until I saw how much work still needed to be done. The Second Coxswain is responsible for the condition of the upper deck and the casing. That means everything from painting the casing and the fin to ordering and stowing of all ropes, hawsers and lines. I also needed a supply of paint, brushes, rollers and solvents to take with us. The most difficulty part was finding space to stow and secure everything. Stowing equipment in the cramped confines of a boat was an art in itself, and tripping over dockyard workers as they rushed around to finish up their work didn't help.

I soon made friends with a Canadian shipmate named Bob Lamb who was nearing the end of his enlistment. He was leaving the navy in about a year's time. I was amazed by a rather strange coincidence. Bob owned a new left hand drive Vauxhall and he was taking it home to Canada. It reminded me of my earlier experience in another Canadian owned Vauxhall.

However, telling Bob about my previous accident was a mistake because every time I rode with him he did his best to scare me. It wasn't surprising that I often felt nervous in his car. Then came an even more bizarre coincidence, or was it fate? Returning to the dockyard one morning we rounded a sharp bend and drove straight into the path of a garbage lorry. I couldn't believe it was happening to me again. We collided head on into the side of the lorry. The Vauxhall was a total write off. Fortunately, apart from a few cuts and bruises, and in my case shattered nerves, neither of us was seriously injured. I vowed on the spot that I would never ride in another Vauxhall owned by Canadian submariner.

With the painting of the casing and fin completed, the submarine was gradually beginning to look shipshape. Then one morning as I was walking through the yard to collect some last minute supplies, I was surprised to bump into Michael Foster. Michael said that he was delighted to be based in Scotland, close to his wife and their home in Lochgilphead. As we resurrected some of our liveliest moments at Ganges and on the Taciturn, he asked if I'd heard from Irene. I told him I hadn't heard anything in over a year and considered the relationship was over. Unfortunately I didn't have time to stand gossiping for too long so Michael and I agreed to keep in touch and we moved off in opposite directions.

I thought no more about this brief encounter until we arrived in Faslane about a week later and received a letter from Irene. It didn't take me long to realise that Michael had written to Marie, and she in turn had told Irene.

It was a glowing letter, telling me how excited she was to have found me again, and how excited Lorraine was too. She said everyone was looking forward to seeing me again and that I must visit the next time the boat came to Faslane.

Common sense told me not to go or even to reply to the letter. Unfortunately common sense wasn't something that I had a lot of.

During the first week of September we sailed for Faslane and the West Coast of Scotland. I stood on the casing as we proceeded down the Firth of Forth, and noted that I had now passed under as well as over the Forth Bridge.

The trip took a week and we tested the systems and the equipment as we went. Once we got to Faslane the real trials would begin. Six weeks of hard work with long hours and little rest. It was crucial training for the officers and the crew. Whether we were experienced or just out of training, it was vital that we learned to work together as a team. We carried out countless fire drills, emergency dives and emergency surfacing drills. The training honed our skills, whether firing a torpedo or alluding surface hunters.

The weekend was the only opportunity to relax, but that often depended on what repairs were required.

I was off duty on our first weekend at Faslane, and I decided to visit Lochgilphead. I felt guilty about Eleanor, but I convinced myself that it was just a harmless fling.

I rented a car in Helensburg and I was on the road early on the Friday afternoon. And when I arrived at suppertime I was greeted like I was the returning prodigal son. I was treated like royalty, with hugs and kisses, handshakes and pats on the back.

Irene appeared particularly happy to see me. We went to the usual bars, then on to one of those wild Scottish dances. But the previous long week at sea was taking its toll so I didn't last long at the dance, and we were in bed before midnight. It wasn't long before I was fast asleep.

I left at noon on the Sunday and returned the car to Helensburg. I didn't want to be late getting back on board as we were sailing at 0500 hrs on the Monday morning. The weekend had been short but I had to admit it had been fun. Nevertheless, I made the decision that it would be my last visit.

On my return to Faslane the following weekend I received another letter from Irene. In it she said that it was imperative that I came to see her because she had something very important to tell me. I had no idea what it was but it sounded ominous.

The sea trials were going well and were almost completed, with only two weeks left. We were looking forward to being declared operational and returning to Portsmouth.

The weekend of October 15th was my last chance to visit Irene and find out what was so important. She was at work when I arrived so I parked at the hospital entrance and waited for her to finish work.

When she eventually came out she seemed tense, looking like she would burst into tears at any moment as she climbed into the car. She asked me to drive to a quiet spot where we could talk. I started the car and drove down the lane turning into the Presbyterian Church grounds and parked under the trees. It was already dark with a light rain was falling, the ground was covered in fallen leafs

I shut off the engine and turned to hear what she had to say. Years later I'd look back on this moment as an award winning performance. Irene burst into tears, holding her head in her hands. I had difficulty hearing what she was saying. Through the sobs and the tears she told me that she was pregnant, and that she didn't know what to do. She was too afraid to tell her parents. They had been bitterly angry when she fell pregnant with Lorraine, this time they'd probably throw her out.

"You won't be able to help me, " she sobbed. "You'll soon be far away in Canada. It's my own fault. I should have been more careful. I've only myself to blame. Oh Lord! What will become of me? What will become of my poor wee Lorraine?"

I sat in utter silence, simply not knowing what to say. I was both stunned and surprised to learn that she was pregnant. How could it have happened? I'd always taken precautions. Irene said she'd been careful too, and then she burst into another fit of crying.

Through her tears she said that being careful didn't matter because there was always a risk. She was going to great pains to assure me it was all her fault, telling me I shouldn't feel guilty. But I was in turmoil, and my mind was spinning.

I couldn't think clearly and didn't know what to say. I was starting to feel the weight and responsibility of my actions. I saw myself as guilty, regardless of what Irene said. It never occurred to me to ask how she could be so sure she was pregnant after only a couple of weeks. She continued crying and sobbing and claiming her life was ruined. I was completely unaware of what was happening or where this was leading. I was too naïve to realise that pressure was being applied to push me into making a decision. All I wanted was this to be over, to start the car and leave this depressing place.

I desperately wanted to go for a pint and pretend none of this was happening. Irene was saying I shouldn't worry. It was her problem. Somehow she'd work it out, maybe rent a small flat somewhere. She would raise Lorraine and the new baby by herself. When she went to work her sister Marie would probably look after the baby. Lorraine was starting school soon so she'd manage to cope.

But the 1960's were a time when a man was expected to take responsibility for his actions. A time when a man was supposed to do the honourable thing. Those were the thoughts running through my mind as Irene relentlessly kept up the pressure.

I was struggling. Then, without any real conviction, I blurted out that perhaps we could get married. And immediately I realised I had just said what Irene wanted me to say. And now it was too late. I couldn't take it back. In that instant the atmosphere in the car changed and I was smothered in kisses and hugs. Irene had successfully accomplished her mission.

By the time I returned aboard on Sunday evening the wedding plans were already well underway. She wasted no time in beginning the preparations. I was sent back with a list of things to do. I was to see the Padre on the depot ship and have him call the banns. I was instructed to let her know the minute I had my leave dates. She needed to book the church and the photographer, and send out the invitations etc.

I had to send her money to help with expenses. It was my job to purchase the rings. The Blarney Stone money was dwindling fast. I was caught up in a powerful surge of wedding plans. I was rushing headlong into something that a few days earlier I would not have even considered. Now it was impossible to stop, or even slow the momentum.

I tried to convince myself that everything was okay and I attempted to act like I was excited and happy. But I was hiding behind a mask of bravado while sinking in a sea of despair too ashamed to write to Eleanor. What could I tell her? How could I explain this sudden decision? I wrote to my family telling them the news and knew that Eleanor would know once my letter reached home. It wouldn't take long for John or Noel to pass the latest news on in the street.

On the 26th November I caught the night train to Glasgow. I was on leave until the 10th December. The wedding was set for Saturday the 29th November at 2pm. Irene had arranged for her brother Angus to stand as my best man, and my sisters May and Anna travelled over from Belfast.

I arrived at the church about fifteen minutes before the ceremony was set to begin. The organ began playing the wedding march as I stood at the altar, and I wished I could just disappear. My head was spinning. This was something I did not want to do. As Irene approached down the aisle I was thinking of running out of the church. But my feet remained firmly rooted to the floor.

Ten minutes later I was married.

After the reception we were driven to the hotel in Minard, the same place Michael and Marie had spent their wedding night two years earlier.

On the Sunday morning we caught the bus into Glasgow. Irene had arranged for us to stay overnight with relatives as we were leaving early on Monday for the Stranraer ferry to Belfast.

I awoke the next morning to an empty house. The family had already left for work. When Irene appeared a few minutes later she looked pale and distraught. Tearfully she began to explain how she had miscarried while sitting on the toilet. She went on to describe the tiny body with its little arms and legs. She said she had no choice but to flush the toilet.

I knew less about a miscarriage than I did about the female menstrual cycle, but I did have the sense to suggest that we should go to the hospital for her to be checked over. Irene said no she was okay. She added that the miscarriage was probably caused by the excitement of the wedding.

We arrived in Belfast that evening, and later that night we had intercourse. Incredibly I continued to remain ignorant of what had taken place. Irene's deceitful scheme had worked better than she could ever have imagined. The only thing I actually noticed was the sudden change in her personality. Overnight she had become more assertive and confident, almost to the point of arrogance.

Of course, with hindsight, it was easy explained. The pressure she was under trying to maintain the pretence of being pregnant would have been horrendous. Once the supposed miscarriage took place and she was over that final hurdle, her confidence would have surged back.

Looking back, it's so easy to see the obvious, but in 1963 I never suspected a thing. It was only later that I started to ask question and put two and two together. I know that if I had not been so naïve (perhaps a better word is stupid) I would not have walked into her trap so easily. But in those days it was too shameful to admit that you had put a girl in the family way. I never mentioned it to my family or friends. Perhaps if I had things might have turned out differently.

All that was left for me to do now was to try and make the best of it. I had lost Eleanor, and there was no way back. I had just fallen for one of the oldest tricks in the book.

Chapter 13
Crossing the Atlantic

The morning of January 4th 1964 was bleak, cold and miserable. A few people, mostly family members gathered on the jetty to see the Alcide slip her lines and silently move away towards the North Atlantic. They waved quietly to their loved ones who were lined up along the casing.

As we passed under Fort Blockhouse we came to attention for the salute. Then we proceeded south, leaving the Isle of Wight and the Needles astern. Our last sight of England faded into the mist as we turned away towards the grey open sea.

Our orders were to sail cross the Atlantic on the surface and to rendezvous with a Canadian frigate somewhere off Bermuda. Once there we were to engage in anti-submarine exercises.

During our second day out we ran into the foulest weather imaginable. Crossing the Atlantic in the middle of winter on board a large ship is, to say the least, an unpleasant experience. Crossing the Atlantic in the middle of winter on a submarine, however, is a completely different, almost indescribable, event altogether. The wind had reached gale force eight and the sea had waves that were cresting between thirty and forty feet. The watch keepers on the bridge were soaked through within minutes of going on duty, and the icy seawater constantly cascaded down into the control room to soak anyone unfortunate to be near the hatch. The boat rocked and rolled so much it became too dangerous for the chef to attempt cooking a hot meal. For three days we subsisted on some dodgy soup and questionable sandwiches. Items that were securely stowed before we set sail suddenly broke loose, plates and cups flew off the table and smashed against the bulkhead. Trying to get some sleep was all but impossible.

On a normal surface ship you could usually find a sheltered spot where you could stand outside and breathe some fresh air, but on a submarine that just wasn't possible. So the stench of vomit, body odor and diesel fumes was something you just had to live with. Only the officer of the watch and the lookouts had the opportunity to taste the fresh air. It was hardly a privilege to be jealous of as freezing spray was continually drenching them.

On the morning of our seventh day at sea I'd just finished my breakfast when my name came over the tannoy to report to the bridge. I threw on an oilskin and climbed the conning tower ladder. The weather had improved by this time and the high winds had subsided, but there was still a heavy sea that caused the boat to pitch into the troughs then rise back up on the high crests.

When the Skipper saw me he just pointed over his shoulder. I followed his finger and immediately saw the heavy hawser trailing about fifty feet over our stern. It had broken loose from its stowage during the storm and was now an obvious danger to the boat because the rope could easily snag on the rudder or the screws.

Immediate action was required, and the Skipper asked me if I was okay about going out on the casing to cut the line.

Naturally I said yes. It was my responsibility. I could hardly ask anyone else to do it. The biggest danger was that each time we rolled into a trough the stern became momentarily submerged. We didn't carry such a thing as a wet suit so I bundled up in a sweater and an oilskin trousers tucked into my sea boots. I tied a towel around my neck to keep water from running down my back, and I buttoned up the oilskin coat over it.

Around my waist I had my belt and a sharp knife attached to it by a lanyard. If I dropped the knife whilst on deck I wouldn't lose it. Next I put on a safety harness and an inflatable life jacket. I felt very restricted wearing so much gear. I decided against wearing gloves. I wouldn't be able to work with then on in any case. If I took them off I would probably loose them over the side.

The Skipper promised to do his best to keep the boat steady and he warned me to just cut the rope loose and not to try and retrieve it. He also told me to be quick as the water was extremely cold.

I climbed onto the forward casing through the small door at the front of the fin. It was difficult moving along the narrow side of the fin to the stern section. With only a handrail on the side of the fin I couldn't use the safety harness until I reached the after casing where a steel cable ran the length of the deck attached to stanchions that were spaced roughly ten feet apart. At each stanchion I had to unhook the harness from the cable and snap it back on again on the other side. Seawater constantly washed over the deck as I slowly moved aft.

In order to cut the rope I had to go inside the casing, but first I had to open the deck plates above where the rope was stowed and climb down. It was about four feet down to the pressure hull and almost immediately I was up to my waist in water that was so cold it caused me to gasp with the shock. The icy water instantly seeped through every part of my clothing.

I had to judge the moment when the stern rose up before I ducked under the casing. I located the end of the rope and began furiously cutting at it. The rope was thoroughly soaked and this made it difficult and slow to cut through. I felt the stern begin its slow descent and my fingers were unbelievably cold as I desperately hacked at the last few strands. I was racing to finish before the water flooded in to fill the casing. I lost the race. I just managed to take a deep breath before I submerged under the wave of icy water. It took so long for the stern to rise again I thought I'd either freeze to death or my lungs would burst.

When it did finally rise and the water rolled away from me I spluttered and gasped for air. My body was totally numb by now and trembling uncontrollably. My chattering teeth echoed in my ears. Then just as the cold had almost completely sapped the last of my strength I cut through the last strand of rope. To my extreme relief it parted neatly, slithered away over the side and was gone.

Climbing back out of the hole and securing the deck plates into place seemed to take forever. I could barely feel my hands anymore, they were so cold and numb, and my legs and arms were so heavy and un-wieldy that picking my way back to the fin took an enormous effort. I wasn't even sure that I'd have the strength to hold on when I had to go around the fin. If I couldn't grip the handrail I would surely be washed overboard.

Fortunately someone on the bridge could see the state I was in and when I reached the fin a ship-mate was waiting to grab me and haul me safely back inside the boat. My wet clothing was stripped off im-mediately, and I was dried with towels and wrapped in a blanket. The coxswain handed me a glass of rum, which I swallow down in one gulp. The rush of heat as the alcohol coursed through my body was a won-derful feeling. I was ordered to turn in and allow my body temperature to return to normal. I had no sooner climbed into my bunk and wrapped myself in several blankets when I fell sound asleep. By lunchtime I was fully recovered, and very hungry.

The waters around Bermuda were much warmer as we rendezvoused with a Canadian anti-submarine frigate. It was time for the exercise to begin. Diving stations sounded throughout the boat and the main vents were opened.

Then suddenly, with the fin still visible on the sur-face, an alarm sounded in the control room. The af-ter planes were not responding. They appeared to be jammed.

The dive was quickly aborted and we returned to the surface to find that the after planes had actually suffered some shaft damage during the storm. There was nothing left to do but head for Halifax.

On the 18th January the Alcide sailed into Halifax Harbour and berthed just below the Angus. L Mac-Donald Bridge. We must have looked a sorry sight. We were supposed to be operational and ready for duty after an extensive refit. But in fact we weren't able to dive, and couldn't even provide our own lines to secure alongside.

Our arrival on the shores of Nova Scotia caused me to ponder on a few very obvious questions. One of the first things we needed to replace was the crockery, which was mostly destroyed during our voyage out. The Royal Canadian Navy supplied us with an issue of unbreakable stuff. It made me wonder why the RN hadn't thought to issue such crockery to us in the first place.

Next on my list of requisitions were some new hawsers and lines, but the weather was so cold that before we could go and get them from the bosun's store we had to borrow some heavy winter parkas from our hosts. It was rather embarrassing seeing RN crewmen walking around with RCN stamped in large white letters across their backs.

When you think that various Royal Navy submarines had been stationed in Halifax since 1956, it surely begged the question why the crew were not better prepared for a Canadian winter. Our winter kit consisted of a light raincoat, wool gloves, wool scarf and boots or shoes. Suitable clothing if you were walking about in an English winter. But we had nothing that came even close to being suitable for wearing outdoors in a Canadian winter. And this contributed greatly to the failure of our first attempt to visit the city. Long before we even reached the dockyard gates our feet were soaked and our ears were frozen stiff.

It really was very difficult to understand. For years the Royal Navy had routinely issued its sailors with tropical clothing as part of their kit. So why the Admiralty did not consider that her sailors might also sail into Arctic waters was beyond me.

Grumbling aside, it didn't take the crew very long to adjust, and within days we were sporting a wonderful range of Canadian winter apparel. Over shoes, boots, fur lined parkas, plaid lumberjack shirts and even long wool underwear.

When we were in harbour only a duty watch remained on board the submarine. The rest of the crew were provided with accommodation in the RCN base at HMCS Stadacona in an old wooden two-storey building known as "C" block. It had probably been erected during the war and was located as far from the main gate as one could get. But no one complained because being out of sight and hopefully out of mind was all right with us.

Anyway, it was not destined to be my home for long because we got word that our wives and families would be arriving sometime in early March. This meant that it was time to look for a suitable apartment to rent.

The boat was eventually repaired ten days after our arrival. Once we were operational it was once more back to sea. We spent a lot of time during February working with Canadian anti-submarine frigates. The brief weekends that we had in harbour became a frenzy of apartment hunting. I eventually settled for a two bedroom at Lakefront Apartments in Dartmouth. Next I had to set about finding and purchasing the necessary, and affordable, furniture to fill the apartment.

With several of my shipmates doing exactly the same thing, we were able to compared notes when we got back on board. This helped us to decide on the best places to shop and where to find the best bargains. Someone had discovered a cheap and cheerful furniture store called Glubes down a Dartmouth side street. For the modest sum of three hundred dollars I was able to completely furnish the apartment. The purchase included a living room set, bedroom set and chrome kitchen set. I also bought a single bed and small bureau for Lorraine's bedroom.

Without curtains on the windows or pictures on the walls the place still looked rather bare. But apart from that it was still by far the nicest place I'd ever lived in. The standard of living in Canada was certainly much better than it was back home. In the kitchen there was a full size fridge and a modern electric range. I'd never had a fridge before, let alone a full size one.

The bathroom had a shower with a constant supply of hot water, and it was an absolute luxury. On the kitchen wall there was a telephone, which was something else that I'd never had before. And even though the Lakefront Apartments were quite old and probably considered down market, to me it was a palace.

The next item on my list was of course, a car. Everyone in Canada seemed to own a car. A few weeks before Irene and Lorraine arrived I bought a 1956 Chevrolet four-door sedan. It was a bit rusty in places but I was still very impressed with its fancy dash and automatic gearbox. I remember the car salesman giving me the strangest look when I asked him to explain how to drive an automatic. Like the fridge and the phone an automatic car was another first for me.

While waiting for Irene to arrive I paid a visit to my old friends, Michael and Betty Chislett. Michael had left the RN had moved back to Canada with his family, once in Halifax he enlisted in the RCN. Now they were living in a new and modern married quarter near Shannon Park.

When I told them that I'd married Irene I spotted a moment of disappointment flash across theirs faces. I pretended not to notice and let the awkward moment pass. Michael had warned me so many times, yet here I was, having done the very thing he advised me against.

Irene, Lorraine and the other families landed at Pier 21 on the 14th March 1964.

We had asked our wives to bring with them as much stuff for the home as they could manage; items like bedding, curtains, crockery and such. My shipmate, Pete Evans was renting an apartment in the building next door to me so together we rented a half-ton truck to carry the luggage. When I saw how much we had to load into the truck I knew it had been a wise decision.

I only had a few days with Irene before we sailed out into the wild Atlantic once again. But I have to admit that coming back to port for the weekends with a home to go to was a nice feeling. And the first few months of married life was not too bad. It was nice to have home cooked meals, and it was wonderful to relax in a hot bath while Irene did my laundry.

I began to think that if Irene had a baby it might strengthen our marriage. Every time I returned from the sea I would ask if she was pregnant yet. She'd tell me not to be so impatient, it usually took two months before one could be sure. This struck me as odd, because before we got married she had apparently known in only two weeks.

It was at this time when I first began to have some serious suspicions. I began listening more carefully when shipmates talked about wives or girl friends. It was a common topic of conversation in the mess, especially at tot time. The usual and constant worry for many a young sailor was getting a girl pregnant. This same concern often applied to married men as well, especially if they already had a large family. And these casual discussions around the mess table were often a wonderful font of knowledge in all matters sexual. I listened to stories about pregnant wives or girl friends giving birth or having miscarriages.

I still wasn't absolutely certain that I'd been hoodwinked into this marriage, but the more I heard the more suspect I became.

In July, though, I forgot all about that when Irene told me that she was pregnant. The wonderful news turned my whole life around, and now I had a special purpose. I was excited and impatient all at the same time, which made the summer days drag on so slowly.

Bob Lamb was leaving the Navy soon, and he was waiting for an interview with the Dartmouth City Police Chief. Unfortunately we were unaware that the Chief of Police had decided to visit Bob at home on the same Sunday we had planned a celebration for him in the Stadacona canteen.

We all gathered in the canteen and as usual hauled all the tables together breaking the club rules. Members were supposed to sit four to a table, with no more than two glasses of draft beer in front of them at any one time. By pulling the tables together this was the first rule we disregarded. Next everyone put two dollars in the kitty, ordered the beer and told the bar-man to just keep them coming. When confronted by twenty or thirty submariners in urgent need of a good drink, the bar staff discreetly pretended not to notice our indiscretions.

An hour later, after a lot of singing and copious amounts of beer, it was time to go to Dartmouth to watch our team playing soccer. Six of us clambered into Bob's Pontiac and headed for the main gate. The sentry at the gate stepped out and signaled for us to stop, but encouraged by all the beer we'd consumed, we challenged Bob to keep on driving.

He did, and we roared through the gate with an inebriated cheer of defiance while the startled sentry scattered out of the way. But even in his moment of confusion the sentry still managed to get the licence number of Bob's car and he called the Halifax Police Dept.

We had no idea that the Halifax Police Depart-ment was looking for us, but fortunately we crossed the bridge to Dartmouth and out of their reach with-out being spotted. At the field we began cheering our team on.

Within minutes Bob's wife Margaret arrived look-ing for her husband. She was in a panic having just re-ceived a phone call from the Chief of Police to say he would drop by around three-thirty that afternoon to have a chat with Bob. We wrongly assumed that it had something to do with our escapade at the Stadcona main gate. It suddenly looked possible that Bob might find himself with the City Police sooner than expected, only this time he'd be in their jail.

I decided we should tell Margaret exactly what happened. She wasn't best pleased but she insisted we took him back to the gate to make a groveling apology to the duty officer. After the reprieve and the cancellation of a police hunt we turned Bob over to Margaret. She proceeded to pour lots of strong black coffee into him before ordering him into the shower.

Surprisingly everything went according to plan and turned out okay. Bob became a police officer a few weeks later, and went on to serve with honour for more than thirty years.

Chapter 14
Caroline Patricia is born.

For the rest of the summer and well into the fall we continued with our extensive exercises at sea, and because of that our time ashore was usually short. Our visits to the Stadacona canteen were even shorter because, after the incident at the main gate and the involvement of the police, we'd been banned from the canteen for a whole month.

That particular ban had already expired by the time we returned to harbour, and was no longer a problem. The real problem was that almost **all** of our drinking sessions on Sundays usually ended with a ban. We simply would not conform to the policy of sitting four to a table. It just wasn't natural.

Another one of our habits that always guaranteed a ban was the practice of lining up outside the canteen and marching all the way back to the block singing loudly. Unfortunately such songs as 'We're a Shower of Bastards' and 'Colonel Bogey' were not conducive to the genteel ambience of a Sunday afternoon, especially when they were peppered with our own choice of nautical expressions.

The singing in itself might have been harmless enough, though, had it not been for the fact that we marched right past the Admiral's quarters every time.

Gradually I stopped going to these Sunday sessions unless there was a soccer game on afterwards. Sometimes I actually played, but most times I just watched.

I sold my rusty old '56 Chev and bought a 1959 Singer Gazelle, which was as good as new. It had very low mileage on the clock and was a great little runner. I actually kept it for the duration of my time in Canada.

It had been parked outside our apartment building for months and I'd never actually seen it being used. I met the owner one day and I offered him $200 for it. He was delighted, and the car was mine. All it needed was a new battery and a couple of tires to bring it up to scratch.

In August we set sail again, this time to join in an exercises off the US East coast, and when it finished we paid a visit to New York. The city was as impressive as I had imagined it would be.

Naturally I went to see some of the more famous landmarks, but it must be said that I actually spent more time in the local bars than I did sightseeing. The bars in New York remained open until 4am, then they close for just one hour for cleaning. Reopening again at 5am. The bar hours took its toll on one foolish young sailor, and he actually ended up in hospital. Apparently he'd run out of money and visited a couple of the local blood banks where he sold a couple of pints of blood at $15 per pint. Needless to say we were given a severe warning by the Skipper about the danger of selling our blood, with the threat of disciplinary action should we choose to ignore it. It worked. Having your pay stopped would cost you a lot more than you'd ever get for a pint of blood.

Early in September we returned to Halifax for a couple of weeks while the boat underwent a brief maintenance routine. This required it being hauled out of the water and onto the Dartmouth slips.

It was great for me as I now lived only a few minutes drive from work. Much better than travelling to Halifax during the morning rush hour when the Halifax-Dartmouth Bridge was routinely grid-locked. I usually had to leave my home at least an hour before I was due on board. But for the next two weeks I'd have an extra half hour in bed.

Irene was about five months pregnant by this time, and was beginning to show. We were getting along reasonably well now, and our time together went fairly smoothly. Nevertheless, I was now certain that she had lied to me, and tricked me into marrying her. Unfortunately I couldn't prove it, and if I confronted her about it she would merely deny it. All it would achieve would be another fight, so I decided that it was easier to just let things lie, for now!

On the morning of the 29th September the boat was due to be lowered off the slip cradle and re-floated. But it was a rotten, wet day with a ferocious cross wind. The decision was taken to delay the procedure until after lunch, by which time we hoped the wind would have subsided sufficiently.

Eventually at around 1400hrs the conditions had improved considerably and we began to slowly lower the boat back into the water. As most of the ships company was on official leave, we only had a skeleton crew on board. Helping me on the forward casing was the wardroom steward. We were using the head rope with four turns around the capstan to hold the bow of the boat central to the cradle.

When I first joined the Navy we used steel cables to secure ships, and these were very dangerous to work with. A frayed strand of wire could easily penetrate a glove and cause a nasty wound. Worse still, if a cable should snap it would scythe through the air, slicing limbs from bodies in its wake. Many a sailor was cut in two by these singing cables, and many others had lost limbs.

Fortunately steel cables were no longer in general use, having been replaced by the white synthetic nylon rope which was so much easier to handle, and considerably safer for the person using it.

So that afternoon we were using a nylon rope to hold us in position. Everything was under control and the boat was slowly and smoothly moving down the slipway. We were quite relaxed as we fed the rope out, watching the stern slowly approach the water's edge. Then suddenly, just as the boat was about halfway down into the water, a ferocious gust of wind came out of nowhere and slapped against us with a vengeance. The violence of the movement put an instant strain on the head rope and forced us to take more turns on the capstan just to stay on station. We were only too aware with the stern already in the water if we allowed the bow to shift in the cradle it could capsize the boat demolishing the slipway with it.

In 1964 there was no real data on the performance of these new nylon lines, but we knew that this particular one was being stretched to its limits. It had now become so taut we were in danger whether we held on or let go. The boat was still sliding down, getting closer to the water with every second. The creaks and groans coming from both the rope and the capstan had us cringing with fear. We knew that if we could just hold on for a few more minutes we would be safely back in the water.

Suddenly there was an almighty ping, and the steward and I were flicked off our feet and thrown unceremoniously back across the deck. The steward disappeared into the well of the escape hatch. I careered past him, flat on my back with both hands lashing out as I desperately tried to grab hold of anything that would stop me from sliding over the side and onto the slipway. As I thudded hard against the fin, the wind died down and the boat quietly floated free of the slips.

The steward was the first to recover and he scrambled over to me, sprawled in a heap in a corner. I was badly dazed and unable to focus clearly, not exactly sure of what had just happened. We were both quickly helped below. All the while I was conscious that someone was determined to keep my right arm as still as possible.

It was only when we reached the mess that I realized why—the middle finger of my right hand was completely broken and was lying flat along the back of my hand, attached only by skin.

Probably because I was in shock, I felt no pain from my hands. They merely felt numb, though they were both swollen and badly bruised. The steward was also battered and bruised, with a suspected broken leg.

The hospital in Stadacona was alerted and they told us they would have an ambulance waiting for us when we tied up alongside in Halifax. But it was going to take about forty minutes for us to cross the harbour and berth. In the meantime the coxswain would have to administer what ever first aid he had available.

Traditionally there were only two options for the treatment of medical conditions on board a submarine—codeine or rum! In my case the prescribed remedy was rum. I was unable to grip the glass myself, so the coxswain held it to my lips. I drained the contents in one gulp. By the time we tied up in Halifax I was more than slightly inebriated and my shipmates had to stop me waving my arm around in case the finger came right off.

At the hospital the x-rays revealed that the middle fingers of both hands were broken, and there was also a lot of tendon damage.

Because of the rum I'd consumed the doctor couldn't risk giving give me an anaesthetic. And because of the swelling they could only splint my hands temporarily and put me to bed. When I woke up the following morning I couldn't decide which hurt the most, my hands or my head.

Twice during the following week I had surgery to save my right finger. It never quite returned to its original shape, but at least in was still attached. Having both hands in plaster at the same time presented me with a whole range of difficult situations, and it was then that I realized who my real friends were. Not one of them accompanied me to the washroom...

After three weeks in hospital I was sent home, and told to rest for another three weeks. When the plaster was finally removed I faced a long period of occupational and physiotherapy. I didn't return to duty until the February of the following year.

One good thing that came from my accident: I was going to be at home for the birth of our baby. The doctor suggested it was due in late December or early January. I was on pins and needles all over the Christmas holidays, pacing the floor waiting for Irene to tell me it was time. When the New Year of 1965 arrived I was beginning to think it was never going to happen. Time dragged by with an interminable slowness. My own birthday was approaching. I would be twenty-six on 15th of January and I was thinking how wonderful it would be if the baby was born on the same day.

On the evening of January 14th Irene started to have labour pains. I'd never driven the Gazelle as fast as I did that night, and we arrived at the Grace Maternity Hospital in less than twenty minutes. It was still only 9.30 pm, and I was now willing my baby to hang on for just a few more hours. At least, until one minute after midnight. Alas it was not to be. My beautiful baby girl arrived at twenty minutes to eleven on the 14th January. But it didn't matter one little bit that she came too early for my birthday. She was here in my arms and it was the most precious gift I ever had. Tears ran down my face as I explained to this wondrous little bundle of joy that I was her father. I think I would have held her all night had the nurse not insisted that I give her back.

For months before the she was born I'd pored over the usual collection of baby names. I had initially decided on Rosemary if it was a girl. But later I realized it would probably be shortened to Rosie, and somehow Rosie Rodgers didn't sound quite right to me.

Finally I settle on Caroline, and later added Patricia as her middle name to reflect her Irish heritage. Irene didn't offer much input when selecting the names, she just agreed with whatever I chose.

From the very first moment I saw Caroline I was totally enchanted by her, and I never got tired of holding her. Everything she did fascinated me; the way she smiled, the way she cried, even the way she slept. The first thing I would do when I came in from work was to pick her up. Irene often got upset because she'd only just managed to get her to sleep. I loved rocking her in my arms and singing 'Tis an Irish Lullaby' to her. I was such a proud father, and I never missed an opportunity to tell everyone within earshot how much she looked like me.

But, sadly, all good things come to an end. In late February I was declared fit for duty and returned aboard the Alcide. It was out to sea once more.

When I returned home again after only three weeks I could hardly believe how much Caroline had grown.

One morning in early April, somewhere north of Bermuda, I really believed that my time had come. Without a shadow of a doubt it was the most terrifying incident I'd ever encountered in all my years working in submarines.

I was roughly roused from the tranquility of sleep it was my turn to go on watch. I reluctantly prised myself out of my warm bunk slowly lowering my feet onto the deck. At sea we never undressed, or changed our clothes. I was already set to go straight on watch, paying a quick visit to the head on the way. The boat was running quietly and everything seemed normal during the watch changeover as bleary-eyed submariners dragged themselves to their various stations. I took up my position in the control room.

We were cruising at a steady four knots, one hundred feet below the surface of the North Atlantic. The cold war was in full swing and we were monitoring our designated zone, listening for intruders. Our polite name for the Russians.

Sitting at the fore plane's control, I wasn't looking forward to the next four hours in the stale damp air that was a mixture of body odor and diesel fumes. The harsh white overhead lights hurt my still sleepy eyes.

At approximately 04.30hrs, as the kye (hot chocolate) was brought around, the officer of the watch gave permission for 'one all round'. This was the code for anyone who smoked to light up. Smoking on board a submarine was a necessary, though restricted privilege that relieved all sorts of tense situations. Not least the effect of chronic boredom. The watch was relaxed and the boat was in the capable hands of George the autopilot, which was controlling the course, speed and depth. Nevertheless, we remained vigilant, as George could be notoriously unreliable at times. While keeping a keen eye on the depth gauge, I helped to solve all the world's major problems with my fellow watchkeepers. We debated everything from religion to politics, and all things in between. After a lot of discussion we ended up selecting the best car of the year.

Then around 0730hrs the wonderful aroma of bacon frying in the galley invaded my nostrils and being hungry I was becoming impatient to see my relief. He eventually turned up dead on eight o'clock, and a few minutes later I was heading off to collect my breakfast from the tiny galley, which was located in the after part of the control room beside the engine room door.

Weary after four hours on watch, I leaned against the bulkhead and watched the eggs sizzling on the grill. Then, just as the chef scooped two of them onto my plate beside several rashers of bacon, I felt the deck suddenly shift beneath my feet and angle sharply downward.

'Come on, lad! Wake up and watch your depth!' the officer of the watch yelled as he angrily berated the plainsman who had just relieved me. I smiled to myself because I knew he couldn't blame George for the mishap. It had been shut down after the relief crew came on watch.

But then it quickly became obvious that the sudden plunge wasn't the fault of the crewman either. For some strange reason we were going into an uncontrolled dive, and in just a few seconds we were down to 200 feet. Things were rapidly becoming very serious indeed.

The 1st Lieutenant rushed into the control room and immediately took charge, ordering the 'shut off for going deep' which was instantly broadcast throughout the submarine.

The Captain was asleep in his cabin, which was located above the control room and outside the main pressure hull. 'Going deep' required every hatch inside the boat to be secured shut with immediate effect. This meant that as soon as the lower conning tower hatch was locked down, the Captain was effectively isolated.

But I couldn't think about that as I slammed shut and secured the engine room door, then assisted in closing all the valves that passed through the bulkhead. Back in the control room I reported that this part of the ship was now totally sealed.

Events now seemed to evolve in slow motion as the crew automatically went about their well-practiced routine for sealing the boat for a deep dive. And every eye in the control room was drawn to the rapidly descending depth gauge readings.

As we reached 400 feet the 1st Lieutenant gave the order that we had all braced ourselves for: 'Blow main ballast.'

This would surely correct the uncontrolled descent and allow us to regain buoyancy. The noise of high pressure air screeching into the ballast tanks was a very reassuring and welcome sound.

I stood breathless and motionless, unable to drag my eyes away from the depth gauge as we waited for the boat to level off and start to rise again. I wasn't alone. It seemed that every man in the control room was frozen in time, eyes firmly fixed on the same gauge.

When the blow was completed an eerie, deathly silence fell over the boat, and we held our breath. But it only took a fraction of a second to realise the horrible truth: we were still sinking.

Blowing the tanks had not even slowed us down.

We were well aware that the part of the ocean that we were currently patrolling was almost two miles deep. We would never reach the bottom in one piece. Then as we passed through 600 feet the 1st lieutenant threw his shirt over the depth gauge, and it snapped us out of our trance.

Standing motionless I listened to the first groans and creaks as the hull was compressed under the enormous sea pressure. The desperate feeling of being trapped in a steel tube was terrifying as we continued to sink toward our crush depth. Powerless to do anything, I just stood there and wondered if anyone would ever know what actually happened to us. I thought about Caroline, would they tell her we died bravely? I felt sad that I would never see her, or the rest of my family again. Strangely, I was sad thinking I'd never again see a blue sky or feel green grass under my feet. It was a bit late now, but I asked myself the silly question of why I'd volunteered for the submarine service in the first place. I forced myself to concentrate on the lessons we had learnt during our submarine training. Although the hull of an 'A' class boat was in theory designed to withstand a sea pressure of up to 1000 feet, as a safety precaution it only ever operated on a maximum depth of 500 feet. Of course these were just figures and I wondered what the builders would be thinking if they were here now to attest to the accuracy. Would they take into account the fact that the Alcide was already more than twenty years old, and the hull would surely have deteriorated during that time?

While I was desperately trying to maintain an outwardly appearance of calm, I was actually consumed by a terrifying fear that I'd never experienced before. My head was light and my heart fluttered as it thumped loudly in my ears.

Then suddenly, as we continued to descend, I felt myself relax. I realised that I had absolutely no control over the events that were unfolding all around me. I accepted that fact and a sense of calmness seemed to creep over me.

However, I still wasn't able to release the death grip that I had on a nearby stanchion, even though my hand was hurting from the pain of holding on so tight. Maybe, I thought, I was adding some extra strength to the hull.

Suddenly a voice pierced my silent reverie.

'Bubble rising, sir.'

I was startled, unsure at first that I'd heard correctly. Maybe I was dreaming, and this was what I desperately wanted to hear. However, shifting my weight to allow for a sudden upward sweep of the deck, I knew it was true! The boat had turned, and now it was racing up toward the surface at almost the same speed we had dived a few moments before. Despite the fact that, at this speed, our sonar could not detect any surface contacts that might be directly above us, no one wanted to slow down to check.

When we broke surface the first man out on the bridge was our very relieved Skipper. Being trapped in his tiny cabin, and not knowing what was happening, must have been an even more terrifying ordeal for him than it was for us.

In reality the entire experience had lasted only a few minutes, but for those of us in the control room, watching our whole lives unravel before us in the glass of a depth gauge, those minutes had seemed like a lifetime.

The question that everyone asked when they got their breath back was, 'what happened? What caused such a sudden and uncontrolled dive?'

But I was just happy to be alive and back on the surface. I didn't care what the caused was, and still hungry, my thoughts turned back to breakfast.

Back in the seaman's mess fear had given way to exaggerated bravado and the place was alive with chatter as we relived the recent event. My shipmates were eagerly relating tales of their own worse experiences (supposedly) while serving on other boats.

'On my last boat we hit the sea bed at 800 feet!'

'Oh yeah! On my last boat we sank stern first and we were stuck on the sea bed for hours!'

And so the stories went on. But for me this was the most terrifying experience of my life. I truly believe I'd walked through the valley of the shadow of death that morning, and it was only by the grace of God had I survived.

But what really happened? What caused the steep dive? How deep did we actually go? These are questions I can't answer with any certainty. Perhaps the best theory and the probable caused was an iceberg. Icebergs are generally made up of fresh water, and as they drift into the Gulf Stream they begin to melt creating huge pockets of fresh water.

That morning it's quite possible that the submarine drifted into the remains of an iceberg, and with the sudden difference in the density between salt and fresh water, we immediately became very heavy and dropped like a stone. It was only when we reached the bottom of the fresh water that we managed to regain our buoyancy and take back control of the boat.

How deep we actually went that morning is open to speculation. Perhaps it was somewhere close to 800 feet. Had the berg been a few feet deeper, maybe I wouldn't be telling this story—who knows?

The event was soon forgotten once we arrived at St George's harbour in Bermuda. We were berthed at the same jetty as the Royal Navy's very first nuclear submarine; HMS Dreadnought. Everyone was anxious to view this fascinating nuclear prototype. I couldn't believe how much more space they had compared to us. The Dreadnought boasted a large mess hall that doubled as a cinema, church or general meeting area. The sleeping accommodations were separate and had both shower and head close by. They even had privacy curtains and reading lamps over each bunk. It looked like the submarine service would soon be divided into two separate branches, nuclear and conventional.

Compared to the other islands like Jamaica, Bermuda was a very expensive place to visit. The speed limit throughout the island was a maximum of thirty mph. The local taxis were mainly small British convertibles with a strange looking surrey canopy or sunshade replacing the convertible top. It didn't matter much because most of us couldn't afford to take a taxi. We either had to walk or hitch a lift if we wanted to go into Hamilton. Mopeds were quite cheap to hire, and equally cheap to run. However, since the movie 'Mr. Roberts' no one would rent one to us. All too often, some fool would emulate the scene from the movie where the sailors rode their mopeds off the end of the pier.

Caroline was almost five months old when I got back to Halifax in early May. It was a time of great excitement for me. I couldn't believe how much she'd grown while I was away. The snow was gone and the weather was beginning to warm up.

I arranged with the base Padre to have Caroline Christened in Saint Andrew's Chapel in Stadacona one Saturday morning. The ship's bell was used as the font to hold the holy water. Lorraine was very much taken with her baby sister, and she took the whole event very seriously.

With the improving weather we were able to take Caroline out more often. I bought a small pram/push chair, and Lorraine quickly decided that it was her job to push it. The safety of children in cars wasn't a major concern in the sixties. I say this because I bought a baby seat that hooked over the front bench seat of the car. It had a flimsy seat belt, and a little plastic steering wheel. They were very popular at the time, and many young families used them. The obvious danger was that if you were forced to suddenly brake hard the baby could be launched straight through the car windscreen. Fortunately this never happened to us, and Caroline survived.

How strange the mind works. When I joined the navy in 1955, twelve years seemed like forever. My actual time didn't begin until I reached my eighteenth birthday, and that was when I officially signed on the dotted line and committed my soul to the Navy.

Now it was the summer of 1965, and it suddenly occurred to me that my time was almost up. On the 14th January 1966 my enlistment expired. I was happy in the Navy, but I hadn't really thought about what I was going to do next. Should I leave, or should I re-enlist? Very soon I would have to make a decision.

A major factor in making this decision was my home life with Irene. Since Caroline was born Irene had taken to going out a lot. I only discovered this by pure accident. One day in the mess, during tot time, a shipmate mentioned a great party that had been held at someone's home the previous evening. He asked me if we'd enjoyed it, adding that my wife sure liked to dance.

I had been on duty watch aboard the Alcide that night, but he didn't know that. I realised because he'd seen Irene he'd assumed I was there too. When I got home I asked Irene what she'd got up to the previous evening while I was on duty. Watched a bit of television, she calmly replied, then had an early night.

Members of the Royal Navy have an odd code of honour regarding their shipmate's wives. If a wife runs around when her husband is at sea, it's probably common knowledge among the rest of the crew. But it's never mentioned in front of him in the mess. So under such circumstances I'd be the last person to know what Irene was up to. It put me in an awkward position because I could hardly ask a shipmate if he was having it off with my wife.

Likewise, if I confronted Irene she would just deny it. In the middle of this crisis my Divisional Officer approached me regarding re-enlistment. Naval regulations insisted that service personnel had to be back in the UK six months prior to them being discharged. So if I didn't sign on, I would be shipped home in August.

When I explained this to Irene and told her we'd have to begin packing, she was less than pleased. She didn't want me to leave the Navy. She was happy the way things were. In July, at the ship's dance at the Jubilee Club in Halifax, she began actively campaigning to have me re-enlist.

She actually danced with the Skipper and talked with him about my signing on. Of course I couldn't know exactly what was said between them. However, a few days later he stopped me in the control room to ask if I'd made a decision.

'Your wife seems very keen to have you remain in the service,' he said. Then he proceeded to point out the many advantages of staying in the Navy. He said I was due to be shortly promoted to Petty Officer and reminded me of the extra pay I'd receive with the promotion. If I stayed on in the Navy I'd have a good pension to look forward to upon retirement. It made a lot sense, but because it was what Irene wanted, I continued to resist.

My final sailing in the Alcide could have ended in a monumental disaster. We arrived in Boston for a weekend visit. On the Saturday morning we were all ready to go ashore and were only waiting for the issue of our rum. Just before noon an American Admiral came aboard, and as he passed the seaman's mess on his way to the wardroom he popped his head in and welcomed us to Boston.

After we'd finished our rum we headed up to the gangway, anxious to hit the hot spots of Boston. As we clambered down onto the jetty we spotted the Admiral's large black Cadillac, complete with pennant and driver, parked nearby.

A young marine was sitting at the steering wheel, and when I playfully tapped on the window I didn't really expect him to respond. He did, and I was taken by surprise when he wound down the window and asked me what I wanted.

'Oh! Er, your Admiral said you were to give us a lift to the dockyard gate.'

Six of us gathered around the Caddy, seriously expecting to be told to Foxtrot Oscar. Instead, this kid didn't even blink.

'Well, reckon if the Admiral said so, ya'll better get in,' he said with a deep southern drawl.

I couldn't possibly back down now, so we all climbed into the back seat for the short ride to the gate.

Meanwhile our trot sentry was shitting bricks, wondering how he was going to explain where the Admiral's car had gone. Fortunately we reached the gate in no time at all, thanked our driver and wished him well, and he was back without being missed.

I've always wondered if he ever mentioned this to the Admiral.

I returned to Halifax, having managed to avoid causing an international incident with the United States Navy. At the end of July I received my orders to return to the UK. We sailed for home departing from Montreal to Liverpool via Cunard liner.

Chapter 15
Back To Civilian Life

My three weeks leave was divided between Loch-gilphead and Belfast, after which I had to report back to HMS Dolphin in Portsmouth. Where I was to spend my final few weeks. And it was one of the strangest periods of my naval career. No one was particularly interested in me or what I was supposed to be doing. I had nothing constructive to occupy my time so I wandered around carrying a clipboard trying to look busy.

Whenever I had an opportunity I searched the jobs situation notices in the local newspapers. I remained undecided about what exactly I wanted to do when I finally walked out of the barrack gates for the final time. Police departments and the Prison Services always favoured service personnel, but I wasn't sure if those were for me. I did go for an interview at a local prison in Portsmouth, but after spending just half an hour inside the sky-high walls I definitely knew it wasn't what I saw myself doing for the next few years.

The Navy would grant three weeks leave for training purposes, but only if I could prove I had a job to go to. I asked Dan, to write a letter stating that I'd be working for him in the green grocer trade.

It worked, and I went home to Belfast for three weeks of supposedly studying the finer points of selling fruit and vegetables.

I returned to HMS Dolphin early in November and I was given the job of caretaker at the submarine museum. It was a small museum with only a one-room display. All that was required was a bit of dusting. On display outside the museum there was an eight man midget submarine known as an 'X Craft'. As it was looking rather run down and neglected I decided to give it a fresh coat of black paint. It was a simple job and one that I could drag out until Christmas leave began.

On the 4th January I said my goodbyes to HMS Dolphin. I had been transferred to Victory Barracks in Portsmouth. The final move in my Royal Naval career. Ten days later I walked out through the gates of Victory Barracks for the last time. I was a civilian once again.

I found it surprisingly difficult to re-adjust to civilian life. No more uniform, no more daily routines, no more saluting. And, unfortunately, no more paydays either! My best hope of immediate employment was a six-month Government re-training course in auto mechanics. I applied and requested the centre located at Dumbarton in Scotland. I did this mainly because the waiting list was shorter there, but also because Irene and the girls could remain in Lochgilphead whilst I completed the course.

We moved in with Irene's parents at the end of January. While I waited for the course to begin I searched for a job locally. There wasn't a lot of work to be had in the village, but eventually I found one driving a local coal-delivery lorry.

Of course I didn't realise at the time that driving the lorry was only a small part of the job. We also had to load the lorry with up to two tons of cwt bags of coal. Then off we went to deliver the 1cwt sacks to customer's homes. I soon discovered that there was a clever knack to carrying a 1cwt bag of coal. But until

I managed to master it I usually ended up covered in coal dust from the top of my head right down to my boots. It filtered through my clothes, got into my pockets, and it even filled my socks.

The family were not pleased about this because I needed a bath every evening, and used up most of the hot water washing off coal dust. I finally learned how to balance a sack of coal correctly on my shoulder before tipping it into the coal cellar without covering myself in dust. The only thing keeping me going in this poorly paid and labour intensive job was the fact that it was only for a short time until I started the course.

Mercifully, I received word in early March that the course would begin on the 1st April. I managed to find comfortable lodgings in Dumbarton, within walking distance of the centre.

The training was intense and I had to work hard just to keep up. Nevertheless, it was a great improvement over humping sacks of coal all day. I purchased an old Ford Prefect so I could travel home at weekends. And thanks to the course training I was able to keep it running for the duration of the six months.

In the meantime Irene got her old job back at the hospital. And plans were afoot, plans that I had not been consulted on.

Not only had Irene put our name down for a council house, she had also asked a relative who worked at the local garage about the possibility of finding a job for me there.

I was never asked if it was okay, just told that it had been done, and that I should be pleased. But as my course progressed I became more and more certain I would not consider settling in Lochgilphead.

Although I only lived with Irene's parents for two days every weekend, it was no longer the warm and friendly place of my Navy days. The days of being the young sailor returning to welcoming arms and happy greetings were long gone. Whatever I proposed or suggested was subjected to a family discussion that ultimately was decided by the majority—them! My suggestions were casually dismissed. I had become invisible. My ideas were ignored. *I* was ignored.

It was getting harder and harder to even contemplate spending the rest of my life in that position so, on the very last weekend of the course, just before I took the final test, I dropped my own little bombshell. I announced that I had decided to go home to Belfast and get a job there.

Irene was furious. She insisted that it wasn't what we'd agreed on, that she'd organized everything, planned our lives. She had no intentions of leaving the village, her parents.

But I was equally adamant and said I had made up my mind. I told Irene to do whatever she felt she had to.But regardless of what her decision might be, I was still going back to Belfast. In the end she realised that she had little choice but to follow me.

When we arrived in Belfast Dan rented us his furnished flat. It was above the shop, and the rent was very reasonable, and fortunately it wasn't long before I found a job. It was with the Blue Peter van hire company, and for the next few weeks everything seemed to be going really well. I was enjoying my new job, the flat was very comfortable, and all the shops were within walking distance.

Then one evening when I got in from work, I was treated to a particularly nice supper. The meal concluded with a delicious steam pudding and custard. I must confess I have always had a weakness for desserts with custard.

But the following morning, as I came down the stairs to go to work, Dan was waiting for me. I didn't know it then, but I was about to choke on the previous nights pudding!

Dan asked me to follow him out to the back yard where he lifted the lid of the dustbin. On top of the assortment of rubbish there were two empty pudding cans. He told me that, because he'd had these cans on a top shelf for so long, unsold and gathering dust, they had become part of the furniture. He was so accustomed to seeing them sitting there that he noticed they were gone the moment he entered the shop.

I was mortified and knew immediately what this meant. I didn't know what to say or do, I could apologize and offer to pay for the goods.

But that wasn't the answer. The real issue was about trust, and the obvious question that hung over it. What else had she taken from the shop? Items such as fruit, vegetables that Dan would never miss?

I knew that, because of Irene's thoughtless actions, we'd have no choice but to move out of the flat. I couldn't expect Dan to continue renting to us after this. The bitter feeling of guilt was immediately replaced by a dreadful anger, and I raced up the stairs to confront Irene. I was so exasperated I couldn't get the words out.

Of course she brazenly denied ever taking anything from the shop without paying, and insisted she bought the puddings in a local supermarket. She tried to pretend that the supermarket labels were still stuck on the tins, and anyway it was just a nasty attempt by my family to discredit her. She knew they didn't like her, and they were always making up stories about her.

I was so furious with her that I knew I had to get out of there before I did something I'd regret for the rest of my life. Apart from that I had to hurry to get to work. I couldn't afford to lose my job, not on top of everything else.

I didn't accomplish much at work that day, my mind was too occupied with trying to work out what I should do next, and I was still angry when I arrived home. I braced myself for a confrontation as I climbed the stairs, and I stopped dead when I pushed the door open. The flat was dark and silent.

When I flicked on the kitchen light the first thing I noticed was the note propped up against a cup in the middle of the table.

It was short, and not so sweet.

I'm not staying here to be accused of stealing by your family, I've gone home to Scotland and you can do what you like.

It was signed Irene.

I'm not sure how I felt at that moment. The suddenness of this, such an unexpected change of circumstances, created a whole concoction of emotions. On the one hand, it solved the problem of having to move out of the flat. But on the other I was devastated that she'd taken Caroline away from me and back to Scotland with her.

Should I follow her, try to sort things out, talk to her? Or was this really the end of the marriage? Did I *want* it to be the end of the marriage? I knew that I no longer had any feelings for Irene, and I honestly didn't give a damn what she did, but I couldn't contemplate losing Caroline.

For the next few weeks I continued to live in the flat, and I made a crucial decision. I was not going back to Scotland. I contemplated applying for a divorce, but I wasn't sure about what grounds I had. More importantly, I wasn't sure if I could even afford it.

I started to think about Eleanor, how I used to feel when I was with her all those years ago, how I'd treated her, how I'd eventually let her down. I wondered if she ever thought about me? How would she react if I approached her again? Was there any hope that we could renew our friendship, our relationship?

I planned it right down to the last second. I waited until she was crossing the street on her way home from work one evening, and I accidentally bumped into her. I pretended to be in a hurry and couldn't stop long. I invited her to come over to the flat one evening so that we could have a chat.

She agreed, and arrived about seven o'clock that Saturday evening. We sat in the front room, our armchairs on opposite sides of the fire, and we sipped tea while I told her about all the things that had happened to me over the past few years.

I suppose I started to wallow in my unhappy predicament, and maybe I sounded a bit too sorry for myself too. But if I was hoping for any sympathy from Eleanor I was right out of luck. I didn't get any. In fact she told me that I was the only one who could sort out my own life. No one else would do it for me. That stung me a little bit.

But when she added that, by bringing her to my flat, I had made her look like she was 'the other woman', that really hurt.

We walked back to her house in awkward silence and stopped outside her front door, on the same spot where we'd stood so many times before, back in those happy days of long ago. But this time it felt very different. I sensed that I'd be rejected if I attempted to kiss her, or even if I tried to put my arms around her. Indeed, when she turned to go in the door, she only allowed me a brief peck on the cheek.

The very thought of seeing Eleanor again, of spending time alone with her, had really lifted my spirits and given me hope, a reason to believe in a brighter future. But now, as I walked back to my empty flat, I felt totally shattered. I'd ruined whatever chance I had of being with her and I was disappointed, and once more I was wandering around in an aimless circle.

I had to pull myself together and get my life back on track. I thought of re-enlisting but that would be admitting I couldn't make it as a civilian. This was one of the hardest times in my life.

Then one wet and cold November morning the answer came to me. I was perched on the tailgate of lorry, having a tea break and reading the Daily Mirror, when I saw the advertisement calling for immigrants to come to Canada. This was it, just what I was look-ing for. I knew I'd lost Eleanor, so there was nothing left to keep me here in Belfast. I applied to Canada House, which was on Chichester Street near the city center. Within a couple of weeks my application was processed and approved. I was informed that I would receive my travelling instructions very soon.

On the 18th January 1967, I landed at Pier 21 in Halfax, Nova Scotia where my old friend Dave Fall met me. He and his wife rented me a room in their home. I found a job at Knowlton Motors, a small garage in Dartmouth that specialized in British cars. I was very happy having returned to Canada and life was begin-ning to look brighter. I even ventured out on a couple of dates.

I had no choice but to keep in touch with Irene because I wanted to keep up to date with Caroline's progress and well being. I never once gave up the hope of having Caroline coming to join me some day.

Then in August I received a letter from Irene saying she'd decided to give our marriage another chance. I wasn't at all keen on that idea. For one thing I'd have to foot the bill for their fares to Canada. But, reluctantly, I agreed, only because it meant that Caroline would be coming home. They arrived a few weeks later and Irene got a nursing post at the Cole Harbour Psychi-atric Hospital. But things went off the rails almost im-mediately. We fought constantly. Outside of work we mostly went our separate ways. I suggested we save Irene's wages and try to manage on mine until we'd saved enough for a deposit on a house. She wouldn't hear of it. It was her money and she do as she pleased with it. In the house we fought over everything, especially Lorraine. When I attempted to tell Lorraine to do something, Irene would immediately overrule me. I was frequently reminded that she wasn't my daughter and therefore I had no say in her upbringing. But it was okay for me to provide food and shelter for the family including Lorraine. Then shortly after the Christmas of 1968, we'd had another stupid squabble over Lorraine. Irene announced she was sending her back to Scotland. She did this for no other reason than to prove to me that she could.

In order for Caroline to attend Sunday school, I joined a local church and soon found myself attending the service on a regular basis. I enjoyed the friendly community spirit, and the warm feeling of support. On the work front things were also going well. I'd changed jobs. I was now the foreman at Halifax British Motors. It meant more money, but with it came the frustrating problem of having to creep along through the rush hour traffic on the bridge every day.

One evening, while I was driving along Portland Street, I spotted Irene walking hand in hand with some guy I'd never seen before. I really didn't care, but I was well aware that the situation couldn't be allowed to continue like this. However, while I procrastinated over what I should do about it, the problem resolved itself. I came home to an empty apartment and found that the bulk of the furniture was gone. There was no note this time, not that I needed one. Her absence said it all.

At the end of the month I moved into a small bachelor apartment, and I had to change my job again. I started working in the auto centre at the new K Mart store in Dartmouth. The hours, and the fact that I didn't have to travel to Halifax every day, allowed me much more time with Caroline.

Irene left Caroline with me whenever it suited her. I knew I was being used as a free baby sitter, but it didn't bother me in the least. I loved every moment that Caroline and I spent together. She was growing so fast, and I loved teasing her about her missing two front teeth. We spent many evenings and most weekends together. We visited the wild life parks, went on church picnics, and joined in with whatever else was going on.

Irene never took any responsibility for Caroline when she left her with me. If I had to go to work that was my problem, often I had to ask Margaret Lamb to baby-sit for me.

At the church I spoke with the Rev Byron Howlett about my situation, and thanks to his advice and guidance I began divorce proceedings. Six months later, on the 29th November 1969, I walked down the steps of the Nova Scotia Court House a free man.

The divorce had taken less than ten minutes. Irene wasn't required to be in attendance and I suspect she wasn't upset about that. She was eight months pregnant at the time.

I have difficulty describing how I felt on that day. It was like a huge weight had been lifted from my shoulders. My six-year nightmare was finally over. Amazingly it was exactly six years to the day. I have never forgotten Byron or the people of Wyndhome Christian

Church, for their support and help during those awful times.

That weekend I wrote to Eleanor asking if she would consider marrying me and join me in Canada where we could begin anew. I couldn't afford the fare or I would have gone home in a flash. Certainly I was free of Irene but not free from her debts. She had charge accounts in several stores around the city and unfortunately they were all in my name. But without a doubt the greatest debt I was left to pay was losing Eleanor. She never responded to my letter and who could blame her. What I had done to her six years earlier was unforgivable. I knew that I had lost her forever.

The End

Epilogue

At the end of 1969 I was transferred to a new K Mart store opening in Charlottetown, Prince Edward Island. Just over a year later in 1970 I met Linda a local girl. We married shortly after that, and moved to Ontario.

I gained total custody of Caroline in 1971while working at a K-Mart in Windsor, Ontario. Our second daughter, Susannah May, was born in Sudbury on the 3rd October 1973.

In 1974 we returned to the island to make our home. That's where you will find us today. Linda and I are both retired.

Caroline is married with two beautiful children of her own, Melissa and Christopher.

Susannah May is a teacher working in Newfoundland.

By a strange set of circumstances in late1993 I unexpectedly made contact with Eleanor for the first time since that fateful night in 1966. She was attending the Cancer Treatment Centre at the Royal Hospital in Belfast. During a chat with another patient my name came up.

This was during the time of sectarian violence in Northern Ireland, and I was involved with bringing Irish children to the island for a four-week vacation every summer.

The patient who Eleanor was talking with had a son living on PEI. He knew of me through the Irish children's program. He later called me to explain how his mother had met with Eleanor and gave me her address saying she'd love to hear from me. Sadly we only had time to exchanged two letters. Her last one arrived in early February 1994, after which I heard no more.

I decided to check the Belfast Telegraph obituaries page and sadly learned that Eleanor had passed away on the 1st March 1994.

It was the worst possible news and so very difficult to come to terms with. My first memory of Eleanor began on a day when she was thirteen years old and attending Everton Secondary School.

The day she said, 'Hi Rock.'

I'm privileged to have known Eleanor and to have shared those fleeting moments of her life that was all too short.

I extend my sincere condolences to Eleanor's family and with the greatest respect I have dedicated this book to her memory.

About the Author

Born in Belfast, Northern Ireland on the fifteenth of January 1939, I was the last of six children. We lost our mother on Boxing Day of 1939. The Second World War was just four months old.

In 1942 my eldest sister Lily, and her husband officially adopted me, and I grew up in England. We lived in a variety of places both during and after the war. At age thirteen I returned to live with my family in Ireland.

In October 1954 I began the process of joining the Royal Navy, and marched off to join HMS Ganges the following year. I was sixteen years of age, and completely unaware of what lay ahead of me at Ganges. It was certainly the toughest boy's training establishment in the British Isles

I served for twelve years and travelled the world in both ships and submarines.

In 1967 I immigrated to Canada, first living in Dartmouth, Nova Scotia and later on Prince Edward Island. I married Linda, an Island girl, in 1971.We spent a short time living and working in Ontario before returning to the island to make our home where we raised two wonderful daughters. And today we dote on two beautiful grandchildren, Melissa and Christopher.

I completed a further twelve years in the Canadian Naval Reserve before retiring in 1998.

Linda and I are both retired now and reside on our fifteen-acre hobby farm, with our two dogs and two cats. Over the years I have followed a hobby of antique British cars and I'm presently driving a 1971 Rover TC.

In the year 2000 I began writing my first book, and four years later I published 'Lily & Me'.

I have had several short stories published in a variety of magazines. My first book 'Lily & Me' was recognized at both the LA Book Festival and the NY Book Festival with Honourable Mention.

Another book by this Author
Lily & Me

This is a wonderful story that will take the reader back to a time when the world was at war. Journey with this young boy as he struggles to regain his identity. Feel his pain and grief, tears and happy moments, humour and courage. This is truly a must read book.

Review:
The Ganges Gazette.

When Fred Rodgers contacted me to review 'Lily & Me' I was a bit sceptical because he said it wasn't actually about the Navy at all. It was about his life leading up to his joining the Navy in 1955.

I wondered if it would be of any interest to our members. However, I said I would look at it and I did. And I thoroughly enjoyed it.

Why?

Because I think, whereas Fred's boyhood was certainly different from my own, we grew up in the same era of the 1940-1950's, and I could relate to his description of living during that period. Doodlebugs, schooling, father (in Fred's case step father) returning from the war etc. This is an excellent read and a social history of the times, and I highly recommend it.

Richard Lloyd. Editor Gazette. UK

Independent Review

Art is the expression of emotion that elicits emotion! You certainly achieved that end. I laughed and I cried. I read an enormous number of books a year. It's my hobby my relaxation and I love to learn. You met all of these goals in this book. Thank you. I'm looking forward to the next instalment. You have a delightful talent.

Libby Goucher. Nova Scotia. Canada

Made in the USA